"Linda Joy Myers folds in her experiences as a therapist and creative-writing instructor to sum up, in detail, the complex journey of memoir writing. Her steps are clear, practical, and accurate and will shed light on the road ahead as you put your story on paper."

—Marina Nemat, author, *Prisoner of Tehran: One Woman's Story of Survival Inside an Iranian Prison*

"This book transforms memoir writing into an adventure with a caring and knowledgeable guide. You can safely take Linda Joy Myers's hand through the forests, swamps, cataracts, and meadows of memoir, learning a great deal on the way."

—Gillie Bolton, author, *The Therapeutic Potential of Creative Writing* and *Reflective Practice Writing, Edition 3*

"In this brilliant new book, Linda Joy Myers shows readers how—by example and with examples—to write the truth about their lives in eight clear steps. She covers multiple aspects of the writing process, including overcoming writing blocks, keeping your motivation alive, and the power of writing to heal both the body and the soul. Dr. Myers serves as an extraordinary guide for anyone contemplating writing a memoir, fiction, or nonfiction. *The Power of Memoir* is a must-read."

—Neil Fiore, Ph.D., author, *The Now Habit: A Strategic Program for Overcoming Procrastination and Enjoying Guilt-Free Play* and *Coping with the Emotional Impact of Cancer: Become an Active Patient and Take Charge*

"*The Power of Memoir* presents clear guidance through complex questions about writing the truth, conquering the inner critic, and putting emotional issues into perspective. And Myers offers the fictional tools necessary to write a professional memoir. I recommend it!"

—Sheri McConnell, CEO, National Association of Women Writers and the Global Institute of Associations

"Anyone who has a story they want to tell will benefit from reading this book. Therapists will find it useful for working with clients who want to create a narrative. Above all, Linda Joy Myers has written a book that will make the telling of painful and difficult things safe and manageable for the writer and the people in their lives."

—Kate Thompson, vice-chair, Lapidus UK, faculty member of The Center for Journal Therapy

"*The Power of Memoir* stuns me with its depth of appreciation for the reader's search for personal story. In an authoritative yet caring voice, Linda Joy generously offers a road map to everyone who wants to embark on this creative journey."

—Jerry Waxler, M.S., memoir teacher and author of the blog Memory Writers Network, http://www.memorywritersnetwork.com/blog

"Drawing on her personal journey as a memoirist and her experience as a therapist, Linda Joy Myers has created a richly informative and user-friendly, highly readable, and comprehensive manual. If you are serious about finally telling your story, this book is a must. Let Linda Joy move you toward your goal of writing your life."

—Lucia Capacchione, Ph.D., A.T.R., art therapist, and author,
The Creative Journal and *Recovery of Your Inner Child*

"Building on her rich experience as a memoirist and therapist, Linda Joy Myers offers a path for writing oneself into wholeness, guiding us from memory to the kind of healing that comes from writing one's truth. *The Power of Memoir* is an indispensable resource for anyone who is inspired to write from life's ups and downs."

—Sharon A. Bray, Ed.D., author,
When Words Heal: Writing Through Cancer

"*The Power of Memoir* is unique among the many books available to help aspiring memoir writers. It ranks at the top of the list if only for the clear and easily understood instruction on the craft of writing, and for Linda Joy Myers's compassionately professional guidance on tender topics like defining boundaries for the story and dealing with secrets and family objections. This material is found nowhere else."

—Sharon Lippincott, M.A., author,
The Heart and Craft of Story Writing

"Painful memories can weigh heavily on an individual and for too long a time. As Myers clearly demonstrates, memoir writing done well can have substantial therapeutic benefits. *The Power of Memoir* is a primer on how to lighten our pain—or even unburden ourselves entirely. An experienced psychologist and memoir professional, Myers is well prepared to guide the reader who seeks a way through and beyond the labyrinth of recurring oppressive memories. In these well-crafted pages, accessible to the accomplished writer and the neophyte alike, Myers presents both theory and practical writing and psychological exercises to work through difficulties of the past. A necessary addition to any memoir-writing bookshelf."

—Denis LeDoux, director, Soleil Lifestory Network, and author,
Turning Memories into Memoirs

The
POWER
of
Memoir

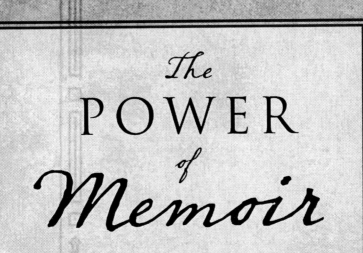

The POWER of Memoir

How to Write Your Healing Story

LINDA JOY MYERS, Ph.D.

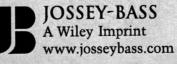

JOSSEY-BASS
A Wiley Imprint
www.josseybass.com

Published by Jossey-Bass
A Wiley Imprint
989 Market Street, San Francisco, CA 94103-1741—www.josseybass.com

Jossey-Bass books and products are available through most bookstores. To contact Jossey-Bass directly call our Customer Care Department within the U.S. at 800-956-7739, outside the U.S. at 317-572-3986, or fax 317-572-4002.

Jossey-Bass also publishes its books in a variety of electronic formats. Some content that appears in print may not be available in electronic books.

Library of Congress Cataloging-in-Publication Data

Myers, Linda Joy, date.
  The power of memoir : how to write your healing story / Linda Joy Myers. – 1st ed.
    p. cm.
  Includes bibliographical references and index.
  ISBN 978-0-470-50836-7 (pbk.)
  1. Autobiography–Authorship. 2. Autobiography–Psychological aspects. I. Title.
CT25.M94 2010
808'.06692–dc22

2009035987

FIRST EDITION
PB Printing   10 9 8 7 6 5 4 3 2

To my children—for inspiring men to heal the generation, and to my sweet grandchildren, Miles, Zoe, and Seth, for showing me that my healing journey has made a difference.

To all the students whose work I've had the privilege to read—you are my teachers. I am deeply touched by your powerful stories and honor your courage and commitment to writing.

In memory of Etty

CONTENTS

Chapter 3   Stories from the Workshops   166

FOREWORD

I f, as some authors suggest, the plot of every memoir is the memoirist's quest to make meaning out of life experiences, then it may follow that one theme of every memoir is the context of family and culture in which the experiences reside.

Our stories shape us, and our families shape our stories. Societies, said Ira Progoff, are "those parts of ourselves that were there before we were." We are each product and process of our own bubbling stew of culture, class, ethnicity, neighborhood, nation, religion, ancestry, DNA. Our most particular and enduring influences are those we are born into.

How remarkable, then, to have a book from a family therapist whose work is to help us tell and write the stories that have shaped us. *The Power of Memoir* represents a sophisticated integration of Linda Joy Myers's decades of clinical experience, merged with her lifetime of creative expression and her own story of triumph over the complexity of circumstance.

Core theories of developmental psychology and family dynamics are concisely reviewed and offered as a pathway into deeper understanding of the context of our lives. An excellent section on why people write memoirs includes reasons not normally addressed in polite company, such as to settle emotional scores, or to expose injustice or abuse. Even potential retaliatory motives are offered dignity and respect, with the understanding that there well might be a shift toward healing along the way.

The eight-step process outlined—from understanding motives to understanding the labyrinthine publishing process—includes a stellar chapter on research, with many free Internet resources and dozens of practical tips on how to fill in historic or cultural gaps. There are also hundreds of story starters, arranged along both narrative and developmental arcs, as well as useful tips for therapists who facilitate individual or group therapeutic writing processes.

As she does in her previous book on memoir, Linda Joy turns over the last section of the book to her students, whose own stories not only provide modeling of the techniques offered, but also make riveting reading.

The cultural anthropologist Angeles Arrien tells of indigenous villages that sit together and share the stories of their days. After each story, whether of feast or famine, struggle or resolve, pride or shame, the villagers nod and say, "Now that's a healing story." May this book guide you to the power that comes from writing your own healing stories.

Kathleen Adams, LPC
Director, Center for Journal Therapy
Denver, Colorado
www.journaltherapy.com

ACKNOWLEDGMENTS

Thank you to my smart and supportive friends in Bella Quattro, my writing group. Without you, and a nudge in the right direction at a writing conference, this book might not have been born. And thanks too for the great food, ambience, and laughter. I look forward to celebrating the joy of creativity many times in the future.

I'd like to thank my agent, Verna Dreisbach, and my editor, Alan Rinzler, for believing in this book and helping it come into being. Thanks to Ron Kane for showing me how to be brave during dark nights of the soul, and how to find the light. I'm so grateful to all the writers I've worked with. Your writing and struggles to tell your truths have been my inspiration.

So many people have shared with me their knowledge, expertise, and support. I can't name you all, but I'm grateful to be part of a community that passionately believes in the power of words, art, and creativity to heal and transform lives. May all our work make a difference in shaping the world into a more compassionate and happy place.

INTRODUCTION

The goal of this book is to help you write the truth about your life, to create a memoir that helps you put unresolved conflicts behind you, heals past wounds, and helps you find meaning, value, and inspiration for your life.

You may ask, "What is my truth—and what will happen if I tell it?" Think about what memories are hidden in the folds of your mind. How do they appear in dreams, haunt you, and invite you to take them from their hiding place? What family secrets make you desperate to find out more, those secrets that whisper the things you need to be able to know to heal the past?

It's important to begin with an understanding of the emotional motivation for writing your memoir. Do you want to set the record straight? Are you writing looking for love, forgiveness, or revenge? Perhaps you want to write the story of your spiritual quest or encounters with extraordinary events or people. This book will address these questions.

As a therapist for more than thirty years, I live in a world of words and stories. Every day I observe how language exposes and hides, breaks open and seals off the writer from her inner truth. Language can be a sword that penetrates stone, or it can build walls. I listen to the stories of my clients, seeking clues to openings and possible change, and turning my ear toward echoes of forgiveness and deeper truths. I do my best to sprinkle the seeds of growth and wisdom that I hope will take root, as I try to protect the garden while praying for gentle rain.

Coming from a family where three generations of mothers abandoned their daughters, it was natural for me to deeply desire that all beings become healed. I was convinced that if words could be said that had never been uttered before, words like "I love you" or "I'm sorry," lives would be changed. I had seen words used to sever the ties of my family, but as I learned to read and discovered books, I saw another way that words could be used.

As a child, I would hide the flashlight under the covers and read for hours, secretly savoring the magic of other worlds, finding that words created new universes where I could learn how to survive the darkness of the family conflicts. Many writers confess the same secrets to me—how literature, poetry, and story have saved them.

After working as a therapist for many years, I began to write my own story, first in journal entries and later in stories, which led to an MFA in creative writing at Mills College. Writing a memoir turned out to be the path to a greater and deeper healing than I would have thought possible. Writing my story and translating it from imagination and memory into words on the page allowed me passage from victim to healing, taking all the separate bits and pieces of my history—my thoughts, feelings, regrets, and hopes—to weave myself whole again.

This book is a culmination and integration of other books, articles, blog posts, and many years of work with clients and students. Along the way, I discovered the groundbreaking research of Dr. James Pennebaker and others who supported what I see in my clients and writing students: writing helps to heal mind and body. His work showed me how to integrate the world of therapy and writing, and to search for others on this same path.

Another important source of inspiration has been Kathleen Adams, director of the Center for Journal Therapy, who trains facilitators and coaches in therapeutic writing. Her work, and my curiosity about the power of writing personal truths, served to launch me into my passion: teaching others how to use personal story and memoir writing to heal. I've also been inspired by Dr. Lucia Capacchione, Denis LeDoux, Tristine Rainer, Christine Baldwin, Deena Metzger, Michelle Weldon, John Fox, Louise de Salvo, Dan Wakefield, Hal Zia Bennett, Susan Albert, and so many others who dedicate their creativity to the art of writing and healing through poetry, writing, and reading literature. Every time I read a memoir or work with students, I'm thrilled all over again to be part of their path of creativity and courage.

When you write a memoir, you embark upon a journey from idea and memory to words on the page. To assist your imagination, you might want to draw from journals or family genealogy or unearth the family photo album. As you begin, you will likely wonder how much of your truth to tell, what's essential to include and what isn't. You might worry about anger or rejection when you grapple with the reality of dark emotions, pain, abuse, and unresolved conflicts. Your memoir may be focused on exploring family patterns or healing from emotional or physical illnesses. It might be a document you want to leave as a legacy to your descendants, or it may be focused on topics you'd like to share with the world. Your stories may be humorous or serious, inspiring or informative. The theme and tone of your memoir will evolve as you begin to write. The most important thing is to start right away!

Most memoir writers are challenged by the task of sorting through the overwhelming amount of detail in their lives. We'll discuss how to organize your work, pick the key events to include, discover important turning points, create your narrative arc, and how to shape your arc of healing. You'll learn about using the tools of fiction, and how to present your memoir to the world. This book will help you begin, develop, and plan your memoir from idea to finished manuscript.

Writing your memoir is an act of courage, an encounter with imagination and memory, and a way to build a bridge from the past to the future. Experience the power of writing your memoir now. Pick up the pen, and listen to that voice inside you as you read on.

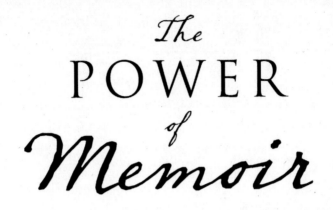

The
POWER
of
Memoir

PART 1

Eight Steps to Writing a Healing Memoir

STEP 1

Understanding Your Reasons for Writing

E ven before birth, we're a part of other people's stories. It's said that we enter the world in the middle of our family's story and become one of the main characters in its drama, immediately woven into the tapestry of family, friends, and community. On our path through life, as in a fairy tale, we encounter wizards, witches, dark forests, and good fairies; we experience joys and challenges, heartaches and hope. Through struggles, failures, and successes, we discover the unique story that is ours alone. We find out who we are and where we are going.

As you muse about writing your stories, you may feel some shyness about putting everything down in black and white, but it's enlightening to encounter the many layers of yourself and your memories, moments that have been captured in a snapshot in your mind, shifting images of perception and consciousness. Writing a memoir is like taking a journey without an exact itinerary. We launch ourselves away from all we know, stopping at stations along the way, only to hop on another train going somewhere we hadn't planned. As long as we're courageous and take note of our travels, we'll benefit and learn from all the new places we visit.

Writing a memoir is an adventure into the unknown and, at the same time, like visiting the comforting old movies of the past that flicker in the parlor, where tea, a fire, and the smiles of our ancestors greet us. Tune in to the whispers of knowledge that are within you, and get ready to write.

Why Write a Memoir

A woman sits across the table from me, her eyes shining. "I have this great story about my mother . . ." she begins. We talk about her idea, and soon it becomes clear that she has a story she wants to tell, filled with the dramas of alcoholism, abuse, absent father, and siblings that need looking after.

"Why are you wanting to write this story?" I ask her.

"Because it was such a hard life, and I overcame all these challenges. I think it will help others." She blinks away tears.

"How much have you written?" I ask.

"I don't know where to start. In fact, I know the family would be upset if I wrote it. My sister told me she'd never speak to me again, and I feel disloyal to my mother." She leans in and whispers, "But isn't it my story?" Her voice has the timbre of strength in it now.

"Yes, it's your story, and you're the only one who can tell it your way. Just begin with some memories in a list, or write down a few small stories you remember."

Her face is pale now, and she turns away. "Oh, I don't know. Maybe it's just for me. I'm so confused about things that happened, and when I write I hear their critical voices, and I feel so ashamed. Maybe I should just forget it." She's looking more crumpled again, and I know that we have some more talking to do.

This scenario is a common one with memoir writers—the struggle between the desire to write and all the issues, conflicts, and worries that come up at the very beginning. When the energy of excitement collides with the sheer wall of fear, guilt, or shame, it's nearly impossible to find the creative flow necessary to write. In future chapters we will examine these concerns carefully and suggest solutions.

The energy of *wanting* to write will drive you through all the barriers, so it's important to hold on to the feeling in your belly that takes over when you think about writing your story, that sense of purpose and inspiration. It's your best friend. And let's look at some of the motivations that drive people to write their memoirs, and how the reasons to write might be part of a healing process. Healing might mean release of old grudges, letting go of hurt feelings, or a sense of freedom and restoration in the body.

Understanding Your Motivation

Here's a list of some of the major reasons why people are motivated to write about their lives.

1. To gain a deeper understanding of yourself and your life
2. To heal the past and create hope for the future
3. To create a legacy for your family
4. To expose injustice or abuse
5. To settle emotional scores—from anger and revenge to acceptance and forgiveness
6. To present a point of view about a controversial issue
7. To share with the world your unique experiences with travel, education, illness and recovery, family, or a spiritual quest

You may identify with some or all of the reasons on this list, so let's take a closer look at possible reasons to write your memoir, and see how they might apply to you.

To Gain a Deeper Understanding of Yourself and Your Life

Writing helps us sort through our memories and experiences, and brings structure to the chaos of our memories. Some memoir writers feel the need to sort out conflicting family histories and put their memories in some kind of order. By telling your story, you deepen your understanding of your family and develop insight into the history and meaning of your life. If other family members wish to disagree, they are free to write their own version of the same events! Later in the book, we'll see how current brain research shows that writing changes the brain and creates new neural pathways that help us heal and find new ways to live our lives. Research has also shown that writing integrates different sides of the brain and helps to contain the chaotic and random nature of memory.

To Heal the Past and Create Hope for the Future

Research by Dr. James Pennebaker and other scientists has proved that writing helps to heal both body and mind, integrating different parts of the brain to heal the effects of trauma. In Step Eight, we will examine these studies in detail. Writing a narrative as a healing practice is now a part of training programs for writers and therapists at the master's degree level, and many therapists recognize writing as a necessary tool in helping to create a new perspective about the past. Writing a story helps to expose the unconscious patterns that keep the client stuck, and offers new inroads into creating a different story for the client to embrace.

To Create a Legacy for Your Family

The story of your unique and special life can be a gift to family members, particularly those not yet born. Think about the many changes that have occurred during your lifetime, all the things you have learned, and the history that is a part of you. Each phase of your life contains a slice of the larger history of the world. You have been part of this vibrant history in some way, as an observer or a participant. Think about the kinds of things your children or grandchildren will never know—how you ran free all day without being nagged to beware of strangers; the way your grandmother made bread or filled the house with song; how you learned to ride a horse; or that you attended political demonstrations.

There are many important events, ideas, and feelings you can pass along from your life to educate and inspire friends and family. These events might include births and deaths, moments of insight and learning, or the ways people lived when you were young. It is up to you whether you include the "darker" or potentially embarrassing parts of your life if you are creating your memoir as a legacy. It depends on what kind of book you want to write, the goals you have, and your audience. Whatever you choose to include, writing your memoir for your descendants can be an act of generosity and love.

To Expose Injustice and Abuse

As a psychotherapist, I encounter many people who are interested in writing about the abuse or injustices they've encountered in their life. Often this writing is for the private purpose of healing themselves, but some people are also passionate about exposing issues to help create change, either now or in the future.

Writing a memoir about abuse in the family might protect other family members from the same fate; describing your experience in an orphanage or foster care might promote more awareness of the challenges other children and adults face, and ways to make things better. When we have lived in extraordinary times and experienced unusual things, we are living witnesses to that history. Holocaust survivors, for instance, can bear witness to stories that otherwise might never be believed. The extensive detail and personal involvement in the survival of horrifying conditions inspired the world to take note. These survivor memoirists created personal history documents and an awareness of the cruelty and bravery of those times, searing the memory of the Holocaust into written history so that it can never be forgotten.

To Settle Emotional Scores

For some writers, the degree of abuse or instability in their child-hoods is so overwhelming and emotionally stinging even after many years, the first reason to write a memoir is to expose the guilty and to set the record straight. They imagine seeing the expression on family members' faces as "the truth" is revealed. They aren't worried about the family reaction, and don't feel guilty or disloyal. Instead, they write in a white heat, fueled by anger and righteous indignation.

In other cases, a spouse may want to get the last word on an ex-husband or wife, so the world will know that they are right and their former partner is forever wrong.

When the book is done, the editing begins. For some writers the layers of editing and rewriting serve to slow down the machinery of revenge, but for others, it remains as strong. I know of an author who didn't tell her family members her memoir was going to be published by a big publishing house, thinking they would not find out, but a neighbor showed up at the door with the book in her hand. The author's family was devastated to see themselves publicly portrayed in a vicious and violent way with no chance to present their own point of view or defend themselves. Perhaps the author was able to resolve her family issues at that point; I don't know. But damage was done. My belief is that the memoirist can write the truth in a balanced way and inform family members so that the memoir is not used as a weapon. Just as easily, it can be a means for healing.

We will discuss in future chapters how you might begin your memoir with anger, and then find your way to other emotional resolutions. There is no one right way to write the memoir, nor a single correct goal. Your words may be more powerful than you know, so it's important to use them carefully.

To Present a Point of View About Controversial Issues

Did you march on Washington, fight in Vietnam, or assist a famous politician? Perhaps you traveled to Africa or grew up in an orphanage, worked in the slums of Calcutta, or spent twenty years as a nun. You might have lived in the closet and been ashamed to be gay or lesbian, and finally now you want to tell the story of how you came out and found your identity. Writing about your experiences can help you to investigate more fully the nature of what happened and simultaneously inform others of events and circumstances that will educate the audience and enlarge their world. Your personal history statements of how you lived in your own skin are powerful, even if they are challenging for you to write about. However, if you are motivated to share your story, it can be a guiding light to inspire others who are struggling with similar issues in their lives.

To Share Your Recovery from Illness or Addiction, or Write About a Spiritual Transformation

When you have gone through something as challenging as recovery from an illness or an addiction, you might have learned many lessons along the way that can help others. Your story can be a cautionary tale—"don't do as I did"—or an instructive manual about how to go through the steps from being lost to finding yourself, from despair to hope and healing, and establishing a new life.

You might view this recovery process as a spiritual quest, or you may have another spiritual journey that you want to share—your experiences with religion, miracles, gurus, and teachers. Writing stories of recovery is a way to sort out the complexities of a process that you might not have understood and integrate it further in your psyche. After it is written, you might discover your story has a universal appeal, and can be a guide for others on a similar path of searching for how to come to terms with their own dark nights of the soul and journeys into transformation and healing.

Overcoming Obstacles to Fulfilling Your Motivation

Whatever your motivations to write, you may encounter difficulties and roadblocks. Here are some of the problems that memoirists encounter most frequently.

Problems Getting Started

Many of my clients, students, and other people I know who are strongly motivated to write a memoir have a lot of trouble beginning.

In his book *Zen Mind, Beginner's Mind*, Shunryu Suzuki writes about freeing the mind through meditation, creating the possibility of a fresh and truly open mind. He says that we should look at everything with curiosity and acceptance, and be both vulnerable and strong; be willing not to know everything, to withstand discomfort, and to be humble.

When you write with a beginner's mind, you may see your story through new eyes. Writing your story the way you now see it, not the way it has always been told, can free you from the strictures of a "right" way to view the world. Perhaps you are the one in the family who doesn't agree with the point of view of other family members. You may feel lonely or even crazy under those circumstances. But, this is what you know, this is your truth.

Hearing Critical Voices

Using a beginner's mind gives us permission to write what we don't know and to write what has never been written before. It is a healthy, open approach to writing from your heart and putting the critical voices aside. You know that nagging little voice. It perches on the shoulder of the writer—we call it "the inner critic." It says things like, "Your life is so boring, you don't remember things very well, you can't really write, who do you think you are?" or even more dire pronouncements, such as "You're wrong, that's not the way it was. You're not telling the truth. You don't even understand what happened."

Taming the inner critic is one of the tools you'll need to keep writing your memoir, and in Step Five we'll talk more about how to do that.

Then there is the outer critic. If you have told your family you are writing a memoir, they may have already expressed their concerns. I have met people whose family members have expressly forbidden them to write a memoir!

The voices of the outer critics and the inner critic can conspire to shut down your writing, especially since you are writing non-fiction. Novelists and fiction writers can hide behind what I call "the fictional wall." They can deny many things that readers might take as truth in the novel, but when you write a memoir, you make a contract with the reader that what you are presenting is the truth, as well as you can tell it. This means that you are writing your most complete version of true events and feelings, even to the point of conducting research to explore various levels of truth.

As long as you don't exaggerate, and if you hold to an ethic of writing your truth the best you can, you won't need to worry about the memoir police coming to get you or humiliate you in public, and your publisher will advise you about any legal issues. It is important to create a safe, sacred space around yourself as you write because your creative efforts must be protected. If you fear retribution or attack, your creativity will tuck its tail between its legs and disappear.

How to Keep Writing

Some of us started writing in diaries or journals as children. Then, as now, we poured out our most private thoughts and feelings there. You might have been lucky enough to have a secret place where you could hide your diary away from prying eyes. Or, perhaps you had no privacy, or your family believed that putting feelings or thoughts into words was dangerous or threatening.

When I was thirteen I received a diary with a little key, but I knew the key would not protect me. I found that diary recently, and I had to translate the words—jottings about events—into what my real truths were. I had to keep my real thoughts and feelings secret even in my diary, because my ever-intrusive grandmother would have too much of me if she read it—and I knew she would. I knew early on that the written word could cause lots of problems.

Keeping a journal is an excellent way to let off steam and explore your thoughts, feelings, and memories. There, you write for yourself with no need for structure or even to make sense. You don't need to explain what you mean or describe people's appearances—you already see them in your mind's eye. You don't need to be fair either; you can rant and rave and no one cares. You are free to explore without fear of being censored or criticized. Your journal is a kind of self-therapy with an always available listener.

Kathleen Adams, director of the Center for Journal Therapy in Lakewood, Colorado, has written several excellent books about the process of healing through journal writing and has created structured processes for a safe and measured way to enter potentially painful material. Through her programs, Adams teaches writers how to use journaling as a kind of self-therapy and therapists how to incorporate journaling as a tool in the therapy process.

Freewriting

Another way to go deeply into what you think and feel without censoring is called "freewriting," where the pen does not come off the page for fifteen or twenty minutes.

In *Becoming a Writer*, Dorothea Brande says that "to have the full benefit of the richness of the unconscious, you must learn to write easily and smoothly when the unconscious is in the ascendant."

She suggests that you should write the minute you wake up, as does Julia Cameron in *The Artist's Way*, but you can write any time of the day or night. Just follow the basic rule: keep writing for fifteen to twenty minutes without stopping. Then if you're up for it, do it again for another fifteen to twenty minutes, committing to whatever comes out.

You can write, "I don't know what to say, this is a stupid exercise, my family will be angry, I want to get up and have some coffee." It doesn't matter what you write, only that you push forward with the pen on the page. It is best to use handwriting for this exercise.

To craft a memoir means wrestling with the nature of truth and the muscles of story structure. It means that you travel back in time and come back with treasures of memory that must be strung together like beads on a string. A memoir has the power to reveal deep secrets and to expose long-buried thoughts, feelings, and events to the light of day. Writing a memoir is to whisper your secret truths into the ear of the reader. Writing your truth is freeing, as you let go of the burden of deeply hidden secrets, and let them come to the surface.

Dr. James Pennebaker, a psychologist who conducts research on the healing power of story writing, says this: "A story is a form of knowledge." Story is a means of teaching us more about ourselves. Writing a memoir means that you are diving into the shimmering pool of memories and coming up with something that can be shaped into a story, and in doing so you will learn more than you could have imagined. No matter how challenged you may feel about writing a long work such as a memoir, if you enter the adventure of writing with an open mind and heart, and dedicate yourself to a path of learning and deeper knowledge, you will be rewarded with emotional understanding, and even healing and forgiveness.

The only journey is the one within.

—Rilke

The best way out is always through.

—Robert Frost

Remembering

As you begin your memoir, you will need to create space for writing in your life, a time and a place where you can nurture your spark of desire into a roaring blaze. As you write, think of yourself as a listener and a translator. Focus inward and hear the stories that whisper to you in a low key; tune in to your desire to capture your grandmothers' history, your mother's face, or your father's character. Try to see the roses on the fence or the dog that saved your life. Remember the scent of baking cookies or the roar of a river. As you remember and write, the essence of your story and who you are will be revealed to you. What is necessary is to show up to the blank page with openness and a willingness to commit yourself to write the stories that make you feel alive, that stir your imagination and make you say, "I just HAVE to write that story."

You will be amazed at the process, even transformed.

Writing Exercises

- Name ten reasons why you want to write a memoir.
- List the family members who might discourage you from writing. Then write why you want to develop your memoir anyway.
- Write about how your journal has helped you in your life.

- If you want to use writing to heal or to create change, describe what you want to change. Be specific.
- Make a list of six inner critic voices.
- List five family stories that piqued your interest as a child. Who told them, and where were you when you heard them? What especially drew you to the stories?
- Did you write as a child? What did you write about? Talk about your early writing life and whether you kept up with it or let it fall by the wayside.
- What teachers inspired you or discouraged you in your writing life in the past?
- List ten significant events in your life.
- As you begin to enter the world of memoir writing, spend some time each day with your memories. Close your eyes and bring yourself back to the time and place where you are a smaller, younger version of yourself. Remember the smells, the sights, and sounds, and enter the movie of your life. These moments serve to fill your imagination with images, and guide you toward the deep, inner, personal research that will fill your pages with remembrances.

Next, we turn to all the ways you can bring your past into the present and create a foundation where you can build the structure of your memoir.

STEP 2

Doing Your Research

Every man is a quotation from all his ancestors.
                                    —*Ralph Waldo Emerson*

Writing a memoir should begin with doing our homework, researching the elements of our story. Writing a memoir is like entering a dream of past memories and simultaneously doing an archaeological dig. Sifting through layers of time and history, you find buried rooms, shards of lost artifacts, and surprising treasures. Sometimes you find buried skeletons too! The nature of your dig will be unique, depending in part on the kind of story you are writing.

Most people are not as daunted by writing a memoir about the external world, or experiences where they were the only witness—such as a travel memoir or a political exposé, but when the writing is deeply personal and revealing, the writers must reach deep within memory banks, drawing upon dreams and even nightmares as they mine their memories for stories. I think that when we are writing memoirs about our lives, no matter what the subject is, we discover surprising things about ourselves along the way. A memoir is a document of discovery. Along the way we uncover and discover secrets and hidden clues to the past and our heritage, while healing past wounds and resolving long-standing conflicts both within us and with others.

Exploring the Elements of Your Story

Doing research is crucial preparation for writing your memoir. Here are some places to look and approaches to take that I've found very helpful. We begin by drawing upon the personal resources that we have, such as photos, family bibles, diaries, recipes, and other family memorabilia.

Photos

One of the best sources for your research will be the family photo album or photo box. If your family is like most families, many of the photos will be tattered and unlabeled, but if you are lucky, you might even know who the people are in the photographs.

A photo is a moment in time captured in the middle of lives that were going on before and continued after the photograph. A snapshot taken in a split second introduces us to these people who gaze at us from another time. It is all we have of our ancestors and our own personal past, and these photos are powerful triggers that help us remember and imagine and write.

Sometimes my therapy clients bring photos to therapy sessions where we look for hidden clues about family dynamics that they may have never noticed before in the photos. Often these can stimulate new memories. One woman brought in a snapshot of herself at the age of two, and later that week had a dream about sexual abuse. Photos often contain powerful messages and clues, if you can "read between the lines" and enter the realm of dream and the unconscious.

The family photos you inherit are a treasure. If you have old photos, look deep into the sepia images, and study the black-and-white snapshots and the later color photos to see what you notice or can imagine about them. Many of you may have gathered more recent photos through digital photography and even cell phones— these may be stored in computers and need to be downloaded or enlarged for easier viewing. In all these images, you will find histories and worlds to help you understand more about who you are and where you came from. Allow your mind to wander and your imagination to take hold as you gaze into the faces who look back at you from beyond time.

Notice what everyone is wearing, the rooms they're in, the houses, landscapes, and weather. Cars tell a tale, as do carriages, horses, cabs, airplanes, and trains. Every detail tells a story that can help you with yours.

> *When you put four edges around some facts, you change those facts.*
>
> —Gary Winogrand

Listening to the Old Stories

My student Barbara told me about the special family moments spent talking with her eighty-six-year-old mother and ninety-year-old father, how she and her sisters gathered at the table with the boxes and albums as they told the old stories.

> *You could feel the power of their memories as we all gazed and murmured over the photos in the evening lamplight. They lifted one photo, then the other, talking fast as they told us about the bread lines during the Great Depression, and how families put gold stars in the windows when their sons were killed during WWII. Shoveling snow in winter, the challenges of just doing laundry—it could take days in the winter time. We laughed at the old cars and the outfits they were wearing. We learned so much about the history of the world, not just their lives. I wished we could have taped these conversations.*

Some family members draw upon old recipes to explore the lore of ingredients and cooking in an old-fashioned style. Others are careful keepers of the family bible, where all the ancestors' birth and death dates are listed in handwriting. With all this raw material, a story begins to take shape, though you may hunger for more details. Personal diaries are a treasure, but many of them contain "just the facts," without much emotion. You may be able to read between the lines to uncover suppressed feelings; through reading a compilation of various diaries, you might uncover hidden nuggets of truth.

Personal artifacts are symbols of what a person loves, treasures, and values, whereas diaries record thoughts and events. Together all these things can help you imagine and create a story from the past.

Interviewing Your Family

Your research should continue with interviewing willing family members, and traveling to locations where your stories are set or where the family came from. Some family members may be more inclined than others to take part in revealing what could turn out to be family secrets. There you may find a treasure trove of original documents and stories that don't appear anywhere else.

Sometimes family members are willing to be video- or audiotaped. Many family members, libraries, and veterans organizations are collecting these valuable taped stories for their archives.

If you are going to be the director of the videotaping, be sure to have the right equipment, sufficient lighting, and see that your subject is comfortable in her favorite chair. You can attach the video camera to a tripod for stability, or you can hold it by hand. The less distracted you are, the better the interview will go. Have your questions ready, and be willing to change topics if your subject launches into an interesting sideline. Some of the best interviews go into areas the interviewer didn't know about beforehand.

To be really free to concentrate on the interview itself, you can hire a professional. Various companies are listed in Google that can take care of all the technical details for you.

Some of your questions will come out of your own knowledge of the family history, or you might encourage other family members to contribute questions they want answered. In some cases, clients attending one of my workshops found it helpful to make a list of questions ahead of time and go over them before the interview. In other cases, being spontaneous was a better approach. Each family has a different style and requirements for a successful interview, and you will discover what works best.

There are two types of family interviews—one is with family members you know, and the other is with someone you have never met before, a virtual stranger, even if you do carry the same DNA. If you are meeting someone for the first time—presumably there would have been a phone call and an arrangement about meeting—the topic of the questions and the way you would interview would have to be off the cuff and spontaneous.

Tune in to their body language when you meet these relatives—do they seem open and are they smiling, or are their arms folded across their chest? If they seem unfriendly or closed, ask the most superficial "fact" questions and leave quickly. If they don't offer you tea, water, or coffee, assume you are an intruder and for whatever reason, they feel threatened. You may be frustrated in your search, but the fact is not everyone wants to dig up the past. Some people can get quite emotional about keeping it closed, secret, or buried, and you will have to accept it if some of your relatives feel this way.

However, most memoirists and genealogists agree with Faulkner when he said, "The past is never dead. In fact, it's not even past."

Uncovering Hot Button Issues

You may have specific questions you want answered that have not been uncovered before and it's possible—even likely when you investigate the past—to run into topics that are "hot button" subjects, such as divorce, illegitimate children, affairs, previously unknown reasons for a death, secret abortions, and stillborn children. If you accidently uncover this kind of information, try to receive it nonjudgmentally and, if the interviewee starts to react emotionally, it's best to stop the interview.

Any kind of genealogy or family research can reveal secrets that have been hidden for generations, so be emotionally prepared for such a possibility. Again, this is where some healing may come in, as revealing the stories could help put some previous shame or guilt to rest, but this very same information could be inflammatory to another family member. Sometimes it is best to allow secrets to lie untouched, but revealing such information can't always be controlled.

You will need permission to tape the interview, and some families will want a release or agreement in writing. They may ask for the transcripts or a copy of the tape for their own records. You can ask if they would be willing to connect with you for online collaboration on the genealogy sites.

Public and Internet Research

Let's look at the public resources that allow you to conduct research from the comfort of your own computer chair.

The Internet is the go-to place for all kinds of research. It's like having a worldwide library at your fingertips. Most of the genealogy research that previously could be done only from original sources can now be conducted on the Internet. Of course, when the documents are missing or seem incorrect, it's still a good idea to search out original documents in local courthouses, libraries, and newspaper archives.

Some of my students have discovered long-hidden facts about psychiatric hospitalization; others have unearthed family stories that were kept secret for decades. Sometimes the dispassionate facts in documents tell more truths than the human families who harbor secrets or shame about the family's past. Later we'll say more on the subject of writing about family secrets, and how to decide what information to make public or keep private in your own archives.

Google

As most of us already know, Google is a powerful search engine that can help us find almost anything. They have expanded their offerings to include searches for text in books, maps—you can even see the entire planet!

For the memoirist, Google is your friend. It's like having a library at your fingertips.

Google Maps   If you want to find a street, town, or city anywhere in the world, you can type it into Google Maps. Photos will come onto the screen of the address you type in. You can zoom in or out, and find the angle where you can best view a building or street. The addresses are not always accurate, so you can scan with the directional arrows until you find the correct address and location. This is a great way to be inspired about the setting and location of your stories. Find the location on Google Maps, and write about what you see and what you remember.

Google Books   Google Books is a search function that allows you to find published books, their references on the Web, and where you can buy them. Some books are reproduced and are available for reading. If you are trying to find a book, Google Books can be very useful.

Google Earth   This program allows you to see the world from multiple points of view, from an eagle's eye view to a close-up. Land masses, oceans, continents, cities, and towns are clearly visible from satellite pictures, which can be an asset to your research if you are locating specific details for your memoir. It's like taking a vacation at your desk to do your research.

Of course, if you're able to take an actual research trip to gather sensual details such as sounds and smells that are not available online, that's a bonus! Be sure to save your receipts if you travel, and ask your accountant how to keep track of expenses spent toward your book. When it's published, you may be able to deduct these expenses.

More Online Organizations

The following are online organizations that can help you with your research. There is a membership requirement for most of these organizations, but some research can be done for free. You are usually able to sign up and create an account which will then allow you to research and keep track of your family tree and to access specific documents.

The Association of Personal Historians lists professionals who can help you with your research and even help you write your story. Visit each of these sites systematically to find out how they can help you, how they differ, and what resources you need. If joining the organization, compare the fee to join to travel time and costs. Much of the information on the Internet can take you very far in your research. The act of finding information and searching for what you need to know can be one aspect of putting old issues and conflicts behind you. The whole process of research can be very satisfying emotionally as well as useful to your story line.

- Association of Professional Genealogists: www.apgen.org
- Association of Personal Historians: www.personalhistorians.org
- Ancestry.com: www.ancestry.com
- Genealogy.com: http://genealogy.com

- Family Tree Maker: http://familytreemaker.com/
- Rootsweb.com: www.rootsweb.ancestry.com/
- Ellis Island Foundation: www.ellisisland.org
- Military Records: www.archives.gov/st-louis/military-personnel

On the Internet, you will find many resources for particular professions, military records, vital statistics, and the census records, which can be researched through 1930. Each state has a vital statistics site where documents may be ordered, and the genealogy sites offer help in getting the documents you need.

Old catalogues such as those from Sears, Roebuck and Co. and Montgomery Ward show artifacts for certain eras, including clothing, furniture, tools, and appliances, offering a rich source of material to make your writing come to life when describing an earlier time. You can find old catalogues in used book stores, online, and in some libraries.

There are many music, automobile, clothing, book, and "decade" sites, such as the Fifties, the Sixties, and so on that show collections of all the memorabilia you might need to recall or draw upon for details that make your story real and believable on the page.

Libraries have great collections of local histories, biographies, and memoirs. Phone books or city directories can give you the history of where a family member lived and worked. I know someone who traced a father's early years through looking him up in a phone book found at the local library. Even when people didn't have a telephone, they had a listing in the phone book or city directory that often included their profession. Surprising details can be learned from unexpected sources. In libraries, local newspapers going back more than a century can be examined for articles and factual information, including the social pages, which tell about the local people, what they were doing, who they visited, and what they were wearing. These are rich sources for family details you might not think of looking for.

One of my students found long-lost connections through the genealogy sites, and another student, who was able to find enough information to decide to go to the original sources, wrote, "I found myself in an old courthouse, and I lifted down these huge books. There I saw the handwriting of my great-grandmother and grandfather. The online documents said they were married when he was twenty and she was twenty-one, but in the marriage document it said, 'Age at next birthday.' So their ages in the original document solved my mystery for me. I stared at the page for a long time, imagining people long dead. It was as if they spoke to me from long ago through their handwriting."

The Story Imagined

Research can produce many of the facts you need to know, and it also allows you to imagine and fill in the story you want to tell, perhaps helping you write a story about a relative you've never met. Writing the imagined story is the way some of my clients fill in the blanks of missed history and story, and help themselves heal. Sometimes what we imagine may be closer to the truth than we would have guessed.

For example, one of my students had been curious about her great-grandfather. She didn't even know his full name, but in her mind, she could hear the cadences of his speech and imagine his life. As she researched the town in Russia that she'd heard relatives mention as the place where her great-grandfather lived, she discovered many pages of history, customs, and details. From this, she could speculate what caused him to send his children to America, yet never arrive there himself. No one in the family knew what had happened to him. The new information helped her enter his story through her imagination, and write it as if through his eyes.

At the end of "Imagining the Past," this student, Sarah Weinberg, talks about how writing the story of her great-grandfather was healing.

*When I wrote this story it made the feeling of connection stronger.
I did research on life in Bobruisk during the time my great-
grandfather lived there. I had a feeling that he wore pehas, as is
customary for Hassidic Jews, yet I did not want to leave this detail
in the story until I knew it was historically accurate. I was
delighted to learn about this kind of detail in my research into the
Hassidic and Yiddish-speaking Jewish communities in Bobruisk.*

*I know there were pogroms in Russia. I needed to research the
time frames in which they occurred to be sure the information
shared in my family while I was growing up was accurate. I found
out that while pogroms took place throughout the 1880s, 1890s,
and early 1900s, the pogrom wave actually avoided Bobruisk
because of a strong resistance movement and the fact that it was a
fortress town and a base for the Russian army. The wave that
flooded many cities and villages in Pale of Settlement destroyed
the mood in Bobruisk, where anti-Semitism was widespread and
Jews were restricted from holding certain occupations. Some Jews
were rich, but many who were poor left the city in droves. In
order to see my relatives living out their lives and feel connected to
them, I needed to learn about everyday life in Bobruisk, what
type of a town it was, and its history. Through doing the research
about my past and my roots to write this story, I was able to fill in
more of the narrative beyond the interviews I'd done, and
experienced a sense of completeness that I had never known
before.*

Sarah's research infused her imagination with another time and
place, impassioned by her deep need to understand those whose
blood was her blood, whose desire to live and survive mirrored her
own. When you are engaged in researching your past, you are
connecting with an ineffable spark, and it is this spark that can
push you toward linking your past and your present in the stories
you write in your memoir.

In all of us there is a hunger, marrow deep, to know our heritage—to know who we are and where we came from. Without this enriching knowledge, there is a hollow yearning. No matter what our attainments in life, there is still a vacuum, an emptiness, and the most disquieting loneliness.

—Alex Haley

Creative Exercises

1. Choose a favorite photo of an ancestor you never met. Explore why this photo speaks to you. What are the details in the photo that gives you clues to who this person was and what they were doing?

2. Write a story from the point of view of that ancestor. Freewrite for twenty minutes just to see what comes out.

3. Make a list of all the questions you would ask a relative about your family if you could interview them. Run this questionnaire by your family members and get their input.

4. Where in the world are the places your ancestors lived? Locate those places on Google Maps or Google Earth, and then write about this experience, including feelings and imaginings about the past.

5. Write a letter to someone in a previous generation. Tell them what they never knew about life after they died.

6. Assign tasks to different family members, such as locating maiden names and researching them, finding addresses, or census and vital statistics records.

7. Create a collage of photocopied pictures of family members. Or, use photos to create a scrapbook that tells the tale of your family. You can add words or not. Use stamps, colorful papers, colored pencils, and cut out words to express your feelings about the people, the places, and the information you have discovered.

Research can be one of the most exciting and active things you can do, and it can become totally addicting. Some people find it hard to start writing because they get so lost in their research. It is best to be very structured in how you obtain your research, and when you have the basics, start writing. In fact, you can write the stories you know and, as you gather information, make lists of what the upcoming stories might be.

After a while, your stories will gather themselves naturally into sets of themes, topics, and time frames. In the next chapter, Step Three, we will discuss how to draw upon the themes you discover to organize and structure your memoir.

STEP 3

Planning Your Memoir

For everything there is a season,
And a time for every matter under heaven:
A time to be born, and a time to die;
A time to plant, and a time to pluck up what is planted;
A time to kill, and a time to heal;
A time to break down, and a time to build up;
A time to weep, and a time to laugh;
A time to mourn, and a time to dance;

—*Ecclesiastes 3:1–8*

A memoir is composed of significant moments, events, characters, and themes selected from your whole life. Because our lives are so full, it can be a daunting task to choose how to focus the memoir and how to tap into memories and choose the ones we want to develop. The third step in our process of writing a healing memoir, therefore, is deciding what to include and what does not belong. When we begin writing, we can get lost in the fragments of memory, thoughts, and images that tumble kaleidoscopically through our minds and in our dreams. Beginning memoirists struggle to gather and pin down these memories, often feeling overwhelmed by the enormity of the task. In this chapter, we will look at steps you can take to capture memories, locate them in time, and discover your themes. At the end of the chapter is a list of developmental questions to help you think about your psychological development over time, and deepen your exploration of your life.

Turning Points

Selecting the major turning points in your life is an important part of this foundational step for writing your memoir. Choosing the major events—events that changed you profoundly—points the way to possible themes and stories to include. Discovering your turning points helps you feel less overwhelmed as you consider your whole life, and gives you a smaller number of important memories to choose from as you sort through the layers of your life's meaning and memories.

One of my students, Kara, was struggling with the focus of her memoir. Wondering how much to include about her childhood growing up as a Mormon girl in Montana. Or should she focus on her adult life—her family or her marriage? Would it be best to go into the story about being a birth mother and giving up her child, or is it too dark and painful a story to go into? Besides, is all that relevant now? Who would read it? These critic voices would slow down her writing, and she had to battle the negative voices in her head.

In her story "Telling That Dark Tale" on page 181, Kara talks about how she resolved these questions.

As you will see, she had tried to escape writing about a guilt-inducing turning point but realized after writing other stories that this significant moment was calling for her to pay attention. She needed to allow the person she had been at that moment to have her voice.

A turning point is a moment of significant change or transformation. A turning point is a time of power and energy, a doorway. A turning point might be meeting someone for the first time, a spiritual awakening, birth, marriage, or death. It could be a crushing, negative experience that changed your life, or a peak experience of joy and harmony. You might not have known at the time if the event was a turning point, but now as you look back, you realize it changed your life profoundly. We experience life—our assumptions, expectations, and perceptions—one way before this turning-point moment, and afterward, we are utterly changed. We can never go back to who we were before that moment. Sometimes we are aware of this moment when it happens, or we might perceive it as significant only from a later vantage point.

Here are some common examples of turning points I've seen among my clients:

- Meeting someone who changed your life
- The birth or death of someone important to you
- A mentor who changed your life
- The discovery of a talent such as music or art
- School events that propelled your life in a certain direction
- The loss of parents, adoption, foster care, or orphanage experiences
- Moments of wonder and awe in nature
- Disasters
- Illnesses
- Encounters with art, books, or music
- Significant travel experiences

Once you have gathered some of these turning points and made your list, you will want to chart them on the time line to create more organization and to help you see the relationship the turning points have to your development through your life.

> Events in our lives happen in a sequence in time, but in their significance to ourselves they find their own order . . . the continuous thread of revelation.
> —Eudora Welty

The Time Line—Charting Your Turning Points

When you chart your turning points on the time line, you're able to see how the stories fit into linear time. The time frame of a turning point story allows you to go forward and backward around that date and event. You can put it into context of the other concurrent events that took place in your family or in the world.

As you write and gather your vignettes and freewrites, it helps to keep charting them on the time line. You will see how events begin to cluster, and these visual clues help you to uncover more memories and notice further associations and layers. The process of uncovering memories, writing, and keeping track of time is a circular one that you will encounter many times over as you write a longer work, such as a book.

The time line helps you to chart the turning points and establishes a way to think about your life. You may want to make several time lines, one for your parents and grandparents, another for your whole life, and another specifically for the time frame of your memoir. Some memoirs cover decades and several generations; others tell the story of just a week or a month of real time.

For instance, Jennifer Lauck's *Blackbird*, her first memoir, covers only a couple of years. In her second memoir, *Still Waters*, she continues the story, then jumps into adulthood and reviews the previous story through her adult eyes. *The Glass Castle* by Jeannette Walls is written in a similar way: the bulk of the story takes place during her childhood, followed by an ending that gives aspects of her adult perspective, almost like an epilogue.

To create your time line, tape several sheets of paper together or buy a pad of large paper. An 18-by-24-inch sheet gives you enough room to develop your time line and have room to note the stories that may cluster around certain time frames. Remember, your memoir will need to eventually find a focus and cover themes from your whole life.

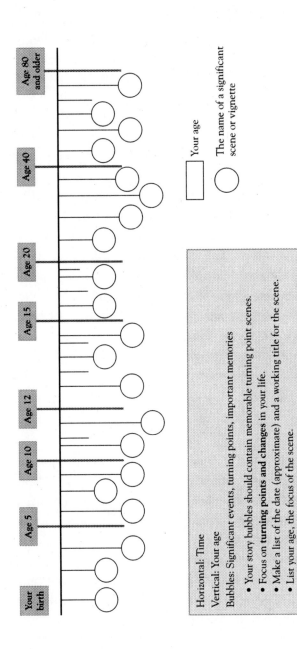

Horizontal: Time
Vertical: Your age
Bubbles: Significant events, turning points, important memories

- Your story bubbles should contain memorable turning point scenes.
- Focus on **turning points and changes** in your life.
- Make a list of the date (approximate) and a working title for the scene.
- List your age, the focus of the scene.
- To use the time line: Choose a turning point and write vignettes in any order
- Tip: Write using sensual details, active verbs.

Figure 3.1 Time Line Template

How to Draw the Time Line

Draw a horizontal line across the paper from left to right to represent linear time. Bold vertical lines demarcate segments, five- to ten-year periods of your life. Use a pencil so you can erase, and don't be afraid to experiment with your drawing. Allow yourself lots of room to fill in the details and time frames that you need. This is meant to be a working document that you can refer to and add to as needed. Most time lines end up frayed and marked up by the end of the process of writing a memoir.

To list your turning point stories, draw vertical lines descending from the horizontal line and draw a circle at the bottom. The circles will contain the title or theme of the turning point story. If you have darker, painful stories, mark them so that you can keep track. Chart all the turning point stories on your list, then turn to other memories that arise, and keep adding these links and story bubbles to the time line. To help you remember more details, choose photos you can copy and paste on the sheet, and family stories that refresh your sense of time and place. This process will continue as you write or do research, and uncover even more memories.

Linear Lists

Now that you have gathered your memories and have begun to bring some order to them, another technique that helps you stay organized is to create lists of stories that you have gathered through your time line exercise and your freewrites. The time line has helped you to put the stories in some kind of chronological order, and now you convert your visual map of stories into a *list*.

The purpose of this list is to create a running document where you can keep track of what you have written and plan to write: the stories you have completed, the stories that are partially written, and those you want to start. You will discover that it is very easy to lose track of your stories if you are writing regularly, or are prolific, so having a clear way to stay organized will help you as you try to choose your themes, and listen to the deeper meaning that begins to arise as you write.

- Put a check next to the stories you have already written.
- Draw a circle to show the stories you have not written, and a half-circle to show the ones you have begun but have not completed.
- Date the completion of the story, so you can keep track of your progress.

After you have gathered quite a number of stories, you will find that they begin to gather into sets of themes, and you'll begin to notice several points that you might use for a focus. In the following sections, we will look at possible themes, and then consider your life passages through a chronological and developmental lens.

Themes

Each memoir has a focal point, a central topic or theme that becomes the unifying force in the book. For example, Pat Conroy's *The Perfect Season* is about his career as a basketball star in high school, and *This Boy's Life* is a classic memoir about coming of age by Tobias Wolff. *Are You Somebody?* by Nuala O'Faolain takes us into a woman's life growing up in another culture, Ireland. Other themes might include abuse or incest, such as *The Kiss* by Katharine Harrison. *Lucky* by Alice Sebold was written in the middle of creating her novel *The Lovely Bones*. She developed writer's block in the middle of the novel, and realized she needed to write about a true traumatic event, a rape. After she completed it, she was able to finish her novel.

Some or all of your stories may be linked to these kinds of themes, including religion, a mother or father's courage, the effects of war, or a life of music. A memoir can be tied together by geographic location or landscape or the healing power of animals and nature, or any kind of pivotal event.

What Is My Story About?

As you look at the following list, note any themes that trigger an emotional response. When you start writing, you may not yet know your theme, but as you continue your project of freewriting, finding turning points, and keeping your lists, you may discover that your stories center around one or more themes. These might include

- Significant relationships
- World events and history and your place in them
- Your emotional life in the past and the present
- The places you lived; the landscapes of your dreams
- Objects and symbols that had meaning for you
- Your philosophy and mental life
- Your behaviors, both positive and negative
- Decisions—the most life-changing ones
- Your dream life
- Yearnings about paths not taken
- Miracles
- Birth and death
- Spiritual or religious themes

The important thing is to not allow the lists to govern all your writing. It's important to continue to allow the freewriting, remembering turning points to free your imagination and keep writing.

A Developmental Model

The following set of questions is meant to help you think about your life in a developmental way. They do not cover all aspects of life, nor will every question be useful to you. But they might help you to think about the important questions.

As you read through the list, mark the questions that stimulate your emotions. You can use the list to randomly choose a topic to write about, or use your emotional reactions to the questions to inspire a freewrite. Exploring your stories and feelings via such emotional triggers can facilitate healing.

Birth and Early Childhood, Up to Age Five

Birth

What do you know about your birth?
Who has told the stories to you?
Were you a wanted child?
What changed in the family after you were born?

Home and Security Base

Who was your major caretaker(s) during those years?
What are your first memories before the age of five?
Do you remember nature, landscape, your house, your room, your bed, a favorite toy or object, siblings, mother, father, grandparents?
Did you live in the same house or apartment, town or city as extended family members?

Social World, Friends, Neighborhood

Did you attend preschool or kindergarten?
Did you have friends your own age? older? younger?
What socioeconomic class did your family belong to during your early years?
What do you remember about your neighborhood or your neighbors?
How about the environment in which you grew up? What do you remember about landscape, weather, and location, such as farm, city, open space, mountains, ocean?
What about experiences with nature or with awe and wonder?

Family

Name the people who surrounded you from birth to age five.

What are the stories about you and who tells them?

What myths do family members tell about you? ("She always . . ." or "He never . . .")

What have you heard about your early toilet training, eating habits, first teeth?

What personality characteristic were you cherished for?

What trait that they found strange or disapproved of became part of the family lore?

Separations and Disconnections

Were you separated from your family during your first five years? Why?

Did you move to a new place?

Were you or your primary caretakers seriously ill?

Were there wars or political upheavals, with relatives or parental figures going to war or leaving home?

What do you know about your parents' and grandparents' attitudes regarding separations?

The School Years, Ages Five to Twelve

Friends and Social Life

What kind of friends did you have? Were they older or younger, same or opposite sex?

What did you like most and least about your friends?

Were you accepted or a loner, shy or gregarious, a leader or a follower?

What do you understand about your attitude toward people, friends, closeness?

School Days

What was your attitude toward school and learning? Did you like it or dread it? Why?

What were your favorite subjects? Do they have any bearing on your life now?

What do you remember about your teachers? Who supported you or saw you as a good learner or person?

Describe your school. What was it made of? Was it old, modern, clean, messy?

How did school affect you emotionally?

Special Training (Music, Sports, Science, the Arts)

How and when did you begin this special interest?

Did you have a special teacher or mentor?

What are your memories of these events?

How did participating make you feel?

Religious or Spiritual Training

Did you attend services at a place of worship?

What were you taught about God or deities?

How did these teachings affect the life of the family at home?

How did these teachings affect you privately?

If you believed in a higher power, how did this belief affect your everyday life at school, home, or on your own?

Your Home

What do you remember about your house?

Describe your favorite rooms and the landscape surrounding your house.

Did you have pets?

Describe the family routine. Did you have chores?
How were weekends different from the rest of the week?
Describe your neighborhood?

Clothes

What was your family's attitude toward appearance?
How did your parents and grandparents dress?
Did you feel proud or ashamed of your appearance?
How do you think you looked compared to the other kids?

Discipline

How did your parents use discipline or punishment with you
and with your siblings?
How were mistakes at school handled at home?
Were you whipped or spanked? How do you define these terms?
Were implements, such as spoons, belts, or switches, used to
punish you?
Were you yelled at or called names?
Was humiliation used as a punishment technique?
How did you feel about any punishment you received?

Play and Creativity

Were you encouraged to be a child or were you pushed to
act older than your age? Were you allowed to play and
daydream?
Describe your play. What did you imagine in your play life?
Did you keep your imaginative games a secret or share them?
Did you draw or pay attention to your dreams and daydreams?

Adolescence, Ages Thirteen to Nineteen

Adolescence is a time to search for and find identity, often by
rebelling against the norm, the family, and society. Certain

aspects of the separation-individuation process of earlier years are repeated, and the adolescent reaches a new level of autonomy.

Sexuality and Your Body

What was your family's attitude toward sex and physical closeness? Was it a healthy, open attitude or one of shame, guilt, and repression?

Were your parents physically affectionate, or was sex repressed or absent in the house?

When did you have "that talk" about sex and reproduction? Who talked to you, and what was his or her attitude?

What did you think and feel about sex and reproduction?

Did you date? As much as or less than your friends?

When you first went out on dates, how did you feel about yourself, your body, the date?

How did you feel about your body changing? Did you feel guilty about sex, your body, masturbation?

Did you talk about sex with your friends?

What did you learn from them?

What was your first sexual experience?

Friendship

If you had a best friend, describe him or her.

Were you social or a loner?

Did you like to spend time with the opposite sex or same-sex friends?

Did you ever feel confused about your own sexual identity?

How did your adolescent friendships help to shape you into the person you are now?

What are some of your favorite memories from that phase of life when good friends mean so much?

School Days

Did your attitude toward school and learning change during adolescence?

How did your life change when you began high school?

Did you have a favorite teacher or mentor in high school? How did he or she affect your life?

How did school affect you emotionally?

How did what happened at school integrate with home life?

How did you answer the question "What do you want to be when you grow up?"

What did you think about growing up at this time in your life? Did you look forward to it, dread it, worry about it, or not think about it at all?

Special Training (Music, Sports, Science, the Arts)

What activities did you engage in and at what ages?

What kind of self-esteem issues did the activities bring up for you?

Write about your favorite memories of participating in these events.

What are your worst memories?

How did participating make you feel? Good, bad, or mixed?

Did your family support your interests? If not, why not, as you understand it now and as you understood it then?

Religious and Spiritual Training

Did your attendance at church or synagogue change during this period of your life? If so, how and why?

How did you discuss your religious training with your parents, friends, and teachers? Did they talk about these things casually or formally, at dinner or by appointment, awkwardly or openly? Were you lectured at or listened to? Was religious training a choice or a requirement?

Did you have mystical or inexplicable experiences, such as intuitive insights or premonitions?

How did your family view death? What did you think about it?

Had anyone in your family or circle of friends died by this point in your life?

If you attended funerals or wakes, how did they affect you?

How did you feel about cemeteries?

Clothes

Were you allowed to wear the current fashions?

How much did your parents control your clothes and style?

Did you have the means to buy your own clothes?

Could you trade with friends?

Were you allowed to express your individuality through your appearance?

For girls, how was the changing of your figure and the need for a bra or sanitary equipment handled? Who was in charge of that information and how was it delivered?

Did you feel proud or ashamed of your appearance?

How did you think you looked compared to the other kids?

Were you proud or ashamed of the appearance of your family when friends came over?

Discipline

When you were a teenager, how did your parents discipline or punish you and your siblings?

How were mistakes at school handled at home?

Were you whipped or spanked? Were implements such as spoons, belts, or switches used? How did you feel about the punishment you received?

Were you yelled at or called names?

Was humiliation used as a punishment technique?

If you were routinely punished, did you rebel and refuse to allow it? How did this refusal change your role or status with adults?

Leaving Home

How and at what age did you leave home? College, marriage, work, running away?

Was your family prepared for this event? Or was there a family crisis about you or your siblings leaving home?

How did you feel about leaving home?

Family Rules, Roles, and Myths

How did your family view itself? As rich, poor, better than others, not as good as others?

Who was closest to you in your family? Who was closest to your parents?

How was power defined in your family? Who had the most?

During stress, did one person side with another? Was this pattern consistent or did the pairings change? Under what circumstances would this pairing occur? Did it happen frequently?

How was your family like or unlike your parents' families?

Is your extended family large or small?

Adult Relationship with Family of Origin

How were holidays handled when you left home?

How did the family respond to your long-term relationship or marriage? Did they participate, send money, become overly involved, or maintain boundaries?

How did you feel about going back home in your twenties,
thirties, forties, and so forth?
What did you miss most after leaving home?
How are you like or unlike your family?
What generational patterns are you aware of?

Adult Life Stages

Courtship, Partnership, Marriage

How did you feel about courtship and marriage?
Why did you marry the person you married?
How did your sexual orientation or identity affect your court-
ship and dating years?

Birth of Children

Did you want or welcome children?
How did having children affect you, your identity, or how you
lived your life?
What was the best and worst aspect of having children?
If you didn't have children but wanted them, how would your
life have been different if you had had them?
If you had them but didn't really want them, how do you feel
about this now?

Work Life and Identity

How did you answer the question "What do you want to be
when you grow up" when you were 10, 20, 30, 40, 50, 60?
Who are you without work roles or work identity?
Is there passion in your work life? A sense of accomplishment?

What would you do when you got up in the morning if it were
the last day of your life?

What does money mean to you?

If you had to choose, would you choose love over money?

Does money bring security for you?

If you could change your life, how would you do it?

Spiritual Changes and Development

How do you define spirituality?

How do you find spirituality in your life now?

Describe the most spiritual experience you've ever had.

Middle Age and Getting Older

What are your thoughts about getting older?

Do you consider yourself older and wiser?

What did you learn from your elders when you were young?

What bits of wisdom do you have to offer younger members of
your family?

Write about your legacy for the younger generations in your
family.

How has your spirituality changed now that you are older?

What are the ten things you must do before you die?

As you think about all the themes and topics that you might
consider for your memoir, you may find yourself wandering through
the remembered halls of the home where you grew up, or leafing
through the family photograph album, musing about your family
and your childhood. You might feel inspired to start writing some
paragraphs or vignettes, but you may also hear in your head the
voice of the inner critic telling you telling you to back off this
memoir-writing project. After all, what will everyone say if you tell
the secrets, if you spill the beans?

But before you put down your pen or close your computer, let's look in depth at the psychology of memoir writing. Because it is so personal, and asks us to probe our deepest feelings, let's investigate how writing a memoir intersects with family rules, loyalty, and our own deepest feelings and beliefs about ourselves.

STEP 4

The Psychology of Memoir Writing

The stories we tell in our memoirs are excavated from a past that shimmers as if in a dream—the dream of childhood and family, the dream of our house and school, of the sidewalks and sandboxes where we once played and created pretend worlds. Woven throughout these origins in place and time is our family, the most significant influence on how we develop psychologically, mentally, and spiritually. There is no way to underestimate the power of the family dynamics we grew up with and our family's strong influence on us, even if we think we can escape it. Therapists often share the joke about a client who moved three thousand miles to get away from his family, only to have to deal with them up close and personal every week in therapy.

Understanding the psychology of the family and the individual helps memoir writers to develop their stories with more nuance and insight. As we grow up, the dynamics in our family of origin seem invisible to us. To us, this is just "how it is." For a child, and even for adults, there is no other perspective but what we are taught in the family home. When students in my classes share their family stories, they are always surprised at the questions and reactions from the other people in the group. Most of them have never before seen or understood their family from another point of view.

For example, my client Elizabeth has been trying to write her childhood and family story for several years, but her memoir is a stop-and-start project. Through writing her stories and hearing the feedback from the class, she began to realize that the family dynamics were not quite what she'd thought, nor were they what was presented to the world on the surface. In public, they appeared to be a united family, with a strong father and graceful mother, but at home things went on in bedrooms in the dark, and the siblings vied for power and stomped on the ones in the lower pecking order. The parents would not make boundaries sufficient to protect the victimized children. Elizabeth found herself caught in a snare of shame and guilt when she became aware of the layers of betrayal in her story. In class, we explored her family dynamics and all the subtle and not so subtle ways they appeared, which helped to support her emotionally in her effort to keep writing. As she proceeded with her stories, she continued to get new insights that freed her from the darkness of her memories. Elizabeth became engaged in the ongoing process toward understanding the under-currents in her family psychology and her own rightful point of view, now that she has found her voice through writing.

Elizabeth grew up in a nuclear family, but many writers who are struggling with their past must confront the atypical ways in which they grew up—often without a traditional family and frequently in situations that challenge how much they really want to remember about their past. They struggle with defining family—does the foster mother or the orphanage count as a family?

What Is a Family and How Does It Work?

The definition of what a family is seems to be expanding as the world changes. The term "family" has traditionally referred to a group of people who had a common ancestor or were related by marriage, including the nuclear family of parents and children; however, it now includes the single parent family, extended family, and large family complexes made up of ex-spouses, stepchildren, and half siblings as well as "brothers and sisters" from foster care. It is a definition in flux.

Nevertheless, all families have a few basic things in common.

As we grow up in the crucible of family, we are always on a continuum of development—becoming who we are with habits, opinions, traits, and belief systems gleaned largely from our family. Understanding the normal stages of child and family development helps us to put our stories in perspective. As we learn about the principles of family interaction and psychology—the roles, rules, and myths that underlie all family systems—we are able to write about our past with greater awareness and self-knowledge, adding new layers of insight that help us to heal. Each new story exposes another layer of clarity and detail to our assumptions about our family and ourselves.

Becoming a Person

As humans, we are composed of four major elements: physical, mental, emotional, and spiritual. We are born helpless and dependent on our parents and caretakers for nurturing, and gradually we learn how to read the family's signals, how to speak, eat, walk, and become more independent. We are shaped by genetics and temperament, fed and watered in the midst of family and community.

After the nurturing stage, we need to be mirrored as the wonderful, unique creature that we are: "Oh, look at Johnny walking. Isn't he cute and wonderful?" During this stage, we learn to have a healthy sense of self and to see ourselves positively mirrored in the delight our parents demonstrate.

There is no such thing as perfect parenting. The psychologist Donald Winnicott posits the concept of "good-enough mothering" to refer to a basic level of nurturing needed for a child to proceed normally into the next stages of development. If this stage of development fails, the child is prone to developing deep defenses against intimacy and trust.

As we grow, we move outward into the community as we attend school and make friends, an environment that gathers us in and reflects who we are back to us—a good or bad student, friend, or team player. The child needs to be able to move forward from family into the larger world and back again for safety and psychic recuperation. Parents themselves proceed through several stages of development, from the nursery stage of high involvement with the child to allowing greater levels of autonomy. The family system must be permeable enough and flexible enough to allow room for everyone to negotiate needs and desires, and to express their personalities. When the family system becomes too rigid, or if there aren't enough psychological boundaries, there will be behavioral and psychological consequences for the whole family.

Family Dynamics

Families tend to maintain a steady state of functioning through an invisible force called "homeostasis," or a balance that is unique to each family. When something happens to disturb this balance, family members try to restore it, to prevent change, and strive to maintain homeostasis by using various tactics. They might use shame and guilt to keep the members in line, or create double bind conditions—damned if you do, damned if you don't—that prevent movement or decision making.

Disturbed and dysfunctional families create a dynamic where individuals can't even comment on the situation without punishment or ejection from the family. Many families find it necessary to hide a great deal of the family story out of shame or guilt, or pride, and commenting on these secrets is forbidden. If a memoir writer uncovers some of the sacred secrets, the family's homeostasis bursts its boundaries. Of course, the memoir writer is to blame for finding out the truth, a subject we'll discuss more in the next chapter, Step Five.

Writing a memoir also can feel threatening to a family when the writer confronts the family's mythical—incorrect—view of itself. When a family's defense system is cracked open, hidden dynamics, beliefs, grudges, and pain come to the surface. Usually each person in a family has a different perspective, seeing events and personalities through a different lens. Families may fight over what "really" happened, what the real truth is. And each view of what happened is also prone to change over time. Some fights are maintained for generations, causing grave and permanent disruption, alienation, and separation.

In every family, there is jockeying for power and control. Who in the family defines reality? Allows comment, movement, and disagreement? Who controls the finances, makes all the decisions? Are personal boundaries respected? Is there a balance between nurturing and independence? These are the kinds of questions I ask as a family therapist to assess the family's functioning.

In a balanced family, the parents, whether there are one, two, or more executives in charge, are at the top of the hierarchy, and maintain boundaries to protect the marital relationship, which is at the heart of the family's stability. The children have their own subsystem and sibling dynamics. When the parent and child systems are balanced—meaning that everyone is able to conduct the business of the family in an environment offering nurturing, protection, and growth—the family functions normally, or in a way that is "good enough." When the systems are out of balance, symptoms develop in the children, such as school problems, sicknesses, fights, bad grades, acting out against authority, and eating disorders. Symptoms in the children can be a sign that things are out of balance in the parental system or in the larger extended family. Sometimes symptoms develop during crises or turning points in the family, such as births, deaths, relocation, divorce, unemployment, and mental breakdowns.

Family Roles

Family members take on roles that become ingrained as part of the family dynamics. Most of us develop these roles unconsciously for a period of time, but in a dysfunctional family the roles become rigid and there is a strong element of inflexibility and fear around change. These rigid systems can persist for decades.

According to Claudia Black, author of *It Will Never Happen to Me*, the children in a dysfunctional family develop roles to handle the imbalance created when parents are not in charge. It's often the eldest child who becomes the responsible one who makes sure that all the homework is done, that food is on the table, and that the other members of the family get to school and work. There may also be a placater, the peacemaker, who tries to stop conflict from erupting, calms things down after a fight, and convinces people to kiss and make up. And there may be a scapegoat, the black sheep of the family, who gets in trouble to distract the family from what is really wrong. Many families also have a mascot, who keeps the family laughing by cracking jokes and clowning.

Another very common role is that of martyr. The martyr gives up his own needs and sacrifices his own happiness to meet the needs of others. The payoff for this is supposed to be gratitude and a bargaining chip for future negotiations: "I gave all that up for *you*." This role of martyr is often transformed into the hero or rescuer role in movies and stories. The hero-rescuer is always busy saving everyone, to the detriment of his own needs. The hero role is often forced upon the eldest child in a family where there is neglect or lack of parental influence. This child will start working at the age of twelve, or make sure that the alcoholic gets up in the morning to get to work. After childhood, the role has become such a part of his psyche that it continues into adult life, eventually creating illness or psychological stress.

Another role is that of victim. Though the victim may have experienced a legitimate injury, the person who takes on this role has an agenda, a need to be seen as one down or as weaker than others, but sometimes this role covers up a hidden power, which is called "the power of the weak." The victim can suck all the air out of the room, and command all the attention, always garnering sympathy for the latest disaster.

Every family member can play these roles, but the children are often forced to adapt to the rules and forces laid down by the parents. However, a parent can be a martyr, clown, or rescuer.

Family Rules

Families have unwritten rules that help preserve the family's functioning and maintain the balance of power. To be accepted and "in," you must obey the rules. If you don't, you might find yourself on the outside—the focus of anger or the target of humiliation and rejection. Maintaining homeostasis—keeping things "the way they have always been"—is a vigorous force for preserving stability, but sometimes the balance needs to be changed for people to grow and reach bigger goals.

As memoir writers begin to write healing stories from childhood and early life, they discover layers of the family rules they had forgotten or perhaps never consciously knew. Writing a dramatic scene with dialogue, character development, and visual description instead of using a distanced narrative brings the writer deeply into the body and experience of a specific time and place. This allows the adult in current time to witness the past with compassion and a new understanding, and to find a new perspective on themselves and the family.

Some family rules that are often discovered when writing such scenes include

- Don't be more successful than we are—or you will shame us.
- Don't be happier than your ___ [fill in the blank: mother, father, grandfather . . .].

- Be successful and make us proud, no matter what it costs you.
- Don't expose the underbelly of the family by saying anything about us.
- Don't air the family's dirty laundry—keep your mouth shut.
- Don't rock the boat—if you follow our rules at all times we will love and accept you.

Family Myths

Family myths are unconsciously held beliefs about the family that help to protect it from shame, guilt, anger, or depression, and to present a good face to the outside world. Myths are similar to the psychological defenses used by individuals. Writing stories that challenge the homeostatic view of the family can get you kicked out of the Thanksgiving holiday and incur anger in those who are unwilling to see the family story in a new way, or to allow you to have your own point of view. Families who demand complete closeness and agreement are called *enmeshed*, whereas families that are so disconnected that they don't provide enough safety or nurturing are known as *disengaged*. Most families are a combination of both, but as your stories reveal the rules, roles, and myths, you will be able to see more clearly how your family fits on the continuum.

Some typical family myths include

- We are better than other people (because of money, status, or rigid beliefs).
- We are more intelligent and talented than anyone else.
- We are poor but proud. (It will be threatening to us if you earn more than we do.)
- We are perfect. (Mistakes are everyone else's fault.)
- We always get along. (You'd better not disagree with us.)
- We never get sick. (If you get sick, you are a weaker person.)
- Uncle Jake is our hero; he can do no wrong. (Don't ever say anything against Uncle Jake.)

Secrets

It's safe to say that there are no families without secrets or conflicts. Some writers may choose to comply with the family rules to keep the silence; others may want to explore deeper truths, believing that exposure heals the wounds that secrets and lies create. No one can tell you what you should or should not reveal in your memoir. Knowing your family as you do, there might be some hot button issues that you know might cause your family to react.

As a memoir writer, you need to ask yourself:

- Who will be injured if I share this?
- Is there a purpose in writing this; will there be a healing?

Naturally, you need come to terms with your own position. Remember: this first draft is for *your own* healing. Secrets hold danger, like a land mine, and they have a profound effect on those who keep them. Energy is required to cover up secrets, and for that reason, they often feel like heavy burdens.

Telling secrets has always caused controversy in our society. For instance, victims are often afraid to speak out about harassment or sexual abuse by family members, priests, teachers, bosses, or anyone in a position of authority. A secret confers power; the person keeping it can completely change another person's life by revealing it. Often a great deal is at stake—reputations, jobs, economic well-being, family unity, and most of all, the way the family sees itself. As a result, the life of the person who tells the secret may also never be the same afterward.

As a family therapist I have been privy to a huge array of secrets that families don't want revealed, that would cause them shame. Some of these secrets may be of concern to you as you prepare to write your memoir:

Illegitimacy, adoption
Murder, criminal behavior, jail sentences

Sexual crimes: rape and incest
Lies about parentage: a "sister" who is really the mother
Money: who has it, who doesn't; how it was acquired
Death, natural or unnatural; wills; inheritances
Elopement, shotgun weddings, secret marriages or divorces
Sexuality, sexual identity
Race, religion, or ethnicity: fear of persecution or rejection
Mental health and developmental issues: the "slow" child kept
    at home, the grandfather everyone keeps an eye on
Drugs, alcohol, and other addictions
Physical illness or genetic problems
Domestic violence

These supposedly hot subjects, possible secrets that might create shame and guilt, can crop up as the inner voice of your critic-censor. It may be difficult for you to decide whether you should listen to the voice saying you are bad if you write that story, that it will surely kill your mother.

James Framo, a family therapist who invites the family of origin to therapy sessions to help resolve couple conflicts, taught therapists how to confront unresolved family shame and guilt. During one of his training workshops, he said that every couple resisted having the family come in and peppered the therapist with reasons: "It will kill them. They'll never speak to me again. My dad will have a heart attack." In every case, none of these dire events occurred. The secret, the anger, the stuck place was gently discussed, opening up communication in the family for the first time in decades.

Our worst fears about how the family might react may come from our child self, fears that are often unfounded in current reality. But only you know your family and their sensitive places. Only you can decide how much to share—but remember, your first loyalty needs to be to yourself, so that you feel free to speak your truths on the page as you write.

Developmental Models of Growth

According to developmental psychologists, character and personality are significantly shaped before the age of five. We do not stop growing at that time, nor are we necessarily stuck with who we were at that young age. Opportunities for growth and healing appear in all seasons of a person's life. As we pass through each stage of development, we encounter opportunities to evolve new strengths, heal old wounds, enhance our creativity and spirituality, and remake ourselves into the best person we can be.

When we write a memoir, we come face-to-face with our former selves, the child we once were, the teenager, the young adult. Through the years we may have forgotten these shadowy parts of ourselves; writing brings them back to us as we listen intently to a voice within. A brief review of the early developmental stages will help us to better understand our younger selves and to draw on them later as we write the memoir. A developmental approach allows us to see ourselves as whole beings. After all, our behavior is the result of many forces: psychological, social, biological, and spiritual.

For the first few months of life, an infant is merged with his mother, unaware of his own body and without a separate sense of self. According to Margaret Mahler, author of *The Psychological Birth of the Human Infant*, the infant needs to feel secure enough with his mother or mother figure (caregiver) in order to separate from her in a healthy way. When the mother figure meets the child's need appropriately, the child proceeds smoothly to the next level of development; however, if there is stress or if the developmental stages are disturbed by physical separation or some other trauma, the child will be vulnerable to psychological problems later in life. The earlier the wound, the more vulnerable the child will be. One of the cornerstones of human development is the infant's need for secure attachment to a caregiver. The child goes through several stages of separation and differentiation during which, ideally, the caregiver supports the child's exploration of the world and provides unconditional love.

Two-year-olds typically struggle with individuation—the process of becoming individuals in their own right, separate from their primary caregivers. The two-year-old's imperious "No" really means, "This is me; I am not you." Through this stormy period, caregivers need to show the child that she is loved, and must provide limits and boundaries with compassion. Two-year-olds may see the world and themselves as all bad or all good, unable to integrate conflicting images and feelings.

By age three, the normally developing child feels secure even when parents come and go. He is now able to integrate conflicting images into a smooth sense of self and others. Physical growth, the acquisition of certain social skills, and cognitive development all help the child understand and interact with his world.

In adolescence the young person repeats certain aspects of earlier developmental stages to integrate them at a new level; this is why teenagers are so passionate about "no" and "yes."

When adolescents leave home, families undergo a major transition. At such times, families show signs of stress and conflict; they must regain balance in a new form. In dysfunctional families, the necessary adjustments may not be made, leading to further stress and to crisis.

In Chinese, the word for "crisis" and the word for "opportunity" are the same. Family therapists agree that a crisis in the family provides an opportunity for new patterns to develop. Every one of us strives to find balance, love, and acceptance as a unique and wonderful being. Healthy family patterns help us meet those needs.

Events and conditions that create stress in the family, such as the physical or mental illness of a family member, alcoholism, frequent moves, poverty, emigration, and war, may disrupt the developmental timetable and force children to grow up too soon.

Certain developmental patterns may also differ from family to family because of varying ethnic and cultural customs. For example, child-rearing patterns in rural Iowa may be significantly unlike those in urban New York. First-generation Chinese Americans may raise their children differently from third-generation Irish Americans.

All of the factors that affect child development and the workings of families need to be considered when writing a memoir to heal.

The Real Self

James Masterson posits his theory of the "Real Self," a deep stream of authenticity and truth that runs at the heart of who we are. He says the Real Self was there before we were born and is the part of us that's balanced and wise and able to love. The Real Self is both a psychological and a spiritual aspect of who we are. Some psychologists and healers call this aspect of self the essential, spiritual, or authentic self.

Masterson posits that this authentic part of us gets covered up as we form defenses that protect us from emotional pain. These defenses include processes such as denial (It didn't happen), projection (It's your fault, not mine), and rationalization (I didn't really want that new job anyway). He says that when the Self is beleaguered by severe, ongoing psychological stress, the "False Self"—a defense mechanism—is established to protect the fragile Real Self from falling apart. The False Self denies our true feelings and creates a façade, or persona, that protects us and helps us to face the world.

A Positive Model of Personal Growth

When thinking of healing, many people don't know what they are aiming for. They ask, "Is there such a thing as a healthy person? Is anyone happy? Are all families unhappy in their own way, as Tolstoy said in his epigraph to *Anna Karenina*?"

Many psychologists have posited models of a psychologically healthy person, and today the psychology of happiness is currently viewed as a way to combat depression and negativity, with its own mix of potential behavioral and cognitive change. However, my favorite model of positive growth and mental health was presented in the 1940s by Abraham Maslow.

Maslow's Hierarchy of Needs

Abraham Maslow developed a theory of humanistic psychology that proposed that people ascend in their development to greater and more sophisticated and particular levels as they are able to satisfy each level of need. Of course, basic survival needs come first, and then comfort, community, and so on, all the way to spiritual transcendence. Deficiencies in the lower-level needs have to be repaired before a person can focus on the higher levels. He believed that humans have a strong need to seek their highest potential for development, and that we as therapists need to hold that potential for people as we work to help them heal. Maslow's hierarchy of needs includes

- Biological and physiological level: the basic survival needs are for food, water, and sleep.

Figure 4.1   Maslow's Hierarchy of Needs

- Safety and security: the need for enough money, a moral compass, family, property, and health help establish a proper foundation upon which to build a life.
- Love, affection, and belongingness: the need for friendship, family, sexual intimacy, and sense of community that supports the emotional and connected self.
- Self-esteem and respect: the need for confidence, achievement, respect for others, and respect by others
- Self-actualization: the need for a sense of spontaneity, problem-solving capacity, lack of prejudice, acceptance, and creativity.
- Spirituality and transcendence: this level was added later in Maslow's life, as he came to understand the need for spiritual connection as part of human development and needs.

Memoir Writing as a Developmental Path (or Actualization)

Writing a memoir can shift the balance in your family and shake up your individual assumptions and beliefs, forcing you to examine the very foundations of your family and your beliefs. Exploring the past and the family through the new lens of story forces all of us to be vulnerable, and requires us to develop our creativity to investigate things that we may have taken for granted before. Through this process, we tap into the love in our hearts and try to have it become more conscious and available. Through the weaving and integrating process, we search for healing and forgiveness as we explore the roots of our identity and assumptions. Exploding myths, challenging the rules that we internalized, and identifying the roles that family members play can be daunting to our sense of security and well-being. The process of writing your memoir creates a circular call and response—the story you write comes from the memories and inner resources that you draw upon, becoming something new that arises from your creativity and your inner wisdom. The story and you, the writer, create a relationship that weaves and develops over time. It grows and changes as the layers of your story, and yourself, emerge and evolve through the levels of your own developmental hierarchy.

All stories keep on developing, if we let them, as they whisper to us what we need to add or take away to shape them into a final form. Sometimes the story demands things from us that we resist, and we must wrestle with them. We will discuss story form in Step Six, but now we are focusing on the creative power of the story itself as it begins to change and heal our lives.

A new psychological relationship is created once we have written the story. We may find ourselves surprised by how we are changed by the story, or that we wrote it at all. The story changes us. "The story is a path of knowledge," says Dr. James Pennebaker in his work about the power of writing to heal.

As you move forward in your quest to write and discover yourself through your writing, it's important to stay open to the process—the horizontal movement in time and through the plot, and a vertical one that invites you to deepen into layers of transformation, as you gather conscious and unconscious details that help you to paint a broad portrait.

Writing Exercises

Apply these questions to your own family and to what you know about the lives of your parents, grandparents, and great-grandparents. You may want to explore generational patterns.

1. What are the stories about the childhood of your parents or grandparents? Were they secure, or did they suffer early separation due to illness, moving, immigration, war, or abandonment?

2. Was there a balance between autonomy and closeness? Write a story about how your development away from the family was

encouraged. Write how you felt you were wanted and acknowledged in your family. If you were not supported in this way, show how that happened in a scene or vignette.

3. Did your parents pay enough attention to you? Show the favorite way they gave you attention. Write about the times when you felt unseen or loved.

4. List the stressors that affected your family. How about your grandparents' generation? Write about these events first from your point of view; then try it from the point of view of your parents or another extended family member.

5. What ethnic and cultural influences affected your family?

6. How was punishment used during your childhood and in the generations that came before? What was the manner of discipline, and who delivered it?

7. How stable was your family—were there many relocations or moves? Could you count on your parents to be there for you? Show how they were there for you, or how they were absent.

8. List five family myths that were needed to protect the family self-esteem.

9. What were the unwritten rules that governed your family?

10. Who played the various roles in the family: the martyr, the victim, the clown, the hero? Write a small story showing each of these roles in action, and how others reacted in turn.

11. In which level of the hierarchy of needs do you locate yourself now, and what are your growth goals as you work on your memoir?

Now that you have a foundation for understanding how psychological change, insights, and self-development evolve through writing a memoir, we'll focus our attention on how these dynamics work on us as we write. We'll investigate next the subject of truth in memoir writing, and how to approach writing about the traumas of the past.

STEP 5

The Dark Stuff

If you bring forth that which is within you,
then that which is within you
will be your salvation.
If you do not bring forth that
which is within you,
then that which is within you
will destroy you.

—*The Gnostic Gospels*

I want to write my memoir, but I'm afraid of the painful, disturbing stories and memories. And besides, if I write about that stuff, my family will get mad at me."

These are the kinds of comments I hear frequently in my work as a psychotherapist and memoir coach, and they're important points to consider when writing a memoir.

The Prevalence of Pain and Abuse in Our Lives

After decades of work as a therapist, I respect the fact that some people have lived more painful lives than others, and that some people really do need to be listened to when they warn me about their memories and the things that get in the way of their writing. I have heard many dark and painful stories of trauma; child abuse; physical, emotional, and sexual abuse; religious abuse; abandonment; rejection; and all manner of lonely, scary times that people spent as children. Abuses occur in adult life as well— rape, physical attacks, and domestic violence. Unfortunately, even adults can be abused by their parents, siblings, or friends.

Sometimes I feel angry that anyone could have been mistreated as a small child, or that anyone would be mistreated at all. Everyone deserves love and positive attention for the marvelous unique beings that they are, but in real life terrible things do happen. There is a continuum, from what we might call mild neglect to horrific abuse, and as a therapist part of my job is to assess the severity of the trauma. As a memoir coach, I do a version of the same thing as I inquire about the nature of the material the person wants to write, especially when they tell me they are concerned about some of their memories.

Preparing to Write

The inquiry I make with writers is not only about childhood, but adult experiences too. I feel it's important to do some kind of assessment with writers, though it won't be as detailed as if I were doing therapy. As a coach I want to know where the hot spots are in the stories, so that I can help the writers manage them, and so that I can guide us around the scary places—navigating our way through any concerns they may have without getting lost in the tangles—as we gain access to the stories they want and need to write.

The kinds of things I ask about include family background, abuse, therapy, and any traumas they may want to avoid writing about. We discuss the issues of the inner critic, shame, guilt, and fear in writing their true stories, and anything else that they feel might get in the way of writing their stories.

How to Overcome Dark Memories That Get in the Way

As we encounter our memories, we find ourselves grappling with "truth," the right to tell our stories, and the voices in our head that get in the way of writing our memoir: the inner critic. However, as we have seen in the previous chapter, Step Four, some of the voices in our head may be the outer critics, the family members who would feel threatened by anyone putting into words some of the family history or sharing the "family secrets."

Getting Unstuck

Some of the questions where memoirists can get stuck:

- What is the truth about my life? Is it what I remember or what other people tell me?
- Does my version of truth have to agree with my family's version?
- Do I need permission from my family to write my memoir?
- I just can't write sometimes—I hear my father's voice threatening me when I pick up the pen.
- My family would kill me if they knew I was writing about them. Should I stop?
- Why should I include all the bad stuff—I've tried to forget about it, and yes, it still haunts me, but why should I wallow in that anymore? I don't want to go there.

Perhaps you can relate to the experience of a colleague of mine: "I have a happy life, things are fine, basically, but these stories are bugging me, the dark ones. They pop up in my dreams, they whisper in my ear. I think about writing them, but then I'm back there, and it's all too much. Still, they won't go away."

There's a lot of research now about the power of writing the truth and the ways in which writing heals. We will be looking at the research about writing and healing in Step Eight, but here we will focus on how to manage the memories and stories that arise, and how to make decisions about the path to take when writing about difficult and challenging emotional events. A little background on this topic will help to clarify why it might be beneficial to write the full range of your stories.

The Value of Revealing Dark Stories

In his book, *Opening Up: The Healing Power of Expressing Emotions*, Dr. James Pennebaker, the premier researcher of writing and healing, talks about the usefulness of writing about emotional events. You will read more about his important research about how writing heals in Step Eight, but even before the studies for which he became known, he was trying to understand how emotional expression heals and if simply expressing feelings is enough. He posits that simple catharsis, an explosive release of emotions, is not enough. Feelings, thoughts, and a new perspective need to be integrated with memories of the events that occurred, which means writing both the "dark" and the "light" stories. This process relieves the pressure of internalized emotions and stress, and promotes a more complete understanding of what happened.

The psychologist Wilhelm Reich, a colleague of Freud's, stressed the importance of understanding how energy gets suppressed and stuck in the body and how this contributes to mental illness and neurosis. He researched the effect of stress and tension on the body, and eventually developed a system of therapy that led to the current body-oriented therapies where breathing and massage are used to relax tension and open up the person to pleasure and happiness again. The goal of Pennebaker's writing exercises and Reich's therapy are the same: expression, release of pent-up tension, and movement toward a new way of being and living that is more open and less based on fear.

Stress and Release

A little about the physiology of stress: when the primitive fight-or-flight system is aroused, powerful chemicals surge through the body so that we can run and defend ourselves against threat. When the threat has passed, the body is still tense and the person maintains a certain vigilance. The goal of healing—release—is to regain balance and allow the body and mind to return to a steady state where relaxation, restful sleep, and normal thinking and functioning can resume. Normalcy also implies a sense of well-being and even happiness.

So we can see that release of tension and free expression of feelings can be helpful to regain a sense of balance. Based on that principle, we'll now address the issues that writers face when encountering their past in dreams and on the page.

Finding the Truth to Write

One of the biggest challenges of writing a memoir is figuring out what your truths are. You need to freewrite without censoring some of the following questions, giving yourself permission to dig deep into the truths of your heart.

After that, you'll need to sort out how to write about them.

Questions to Ask Yourself

These kinds of questions come to mind:

- What are *my* truths?
- How do I know that what I'm writing *is* the truth?
- Do I want to even think about layers of truth in my past?

- I don't want to explore everything. Will I be in control of what I write?

When you decide to write a memoir, you dive into your own movie of the past in your mind, only to realize that your memory is not such a simple thing. You discover that the family may have competing memories about the same event, and you may encounter stumbling blocks and challenges to the concept of "reality" and "truth." Each person's truth is unique; sometimes no agreement can be found in the family.

Discovering the Levels of Truth

We come to realize that there are levels of truth, and that some of these levels have been hidden in our unconscious, only to stream out of the end of the pen as we begin to write. In a family that considers itself "close," the family identity and structure may be threatened by truths expressed by another family member that is different from the prevailing family view. We learned about homeostasis in the preceding chapter, Step Four, and know that the balance must be maintained to bring the dissenting voice in line. Thinking differently and having your own version of the truth is seen as dangerous by members of what we call an enmeshed, or overly close family.

Past pressures to conform and mirror the family, combined with the current attitudes the family may have about your writing, create a powerful inner and outer critic that can stall even the most stalwart and determined writer. But we know that in order to create the memoir that is calling to us, beckoning us, we must solve these problems.

"The truth" is a sacred idea to many people. Many of us were brought up to always tell the truth, and we learned that if you start lying, you have to cover it up with more lies until you don't know the truth anymore. As children we learn that "honesty is the best policy" and that we'll be punished if we lie, so when writers doubt whether their memories are true, they often feel a great deal of guilt and shame as they struggle to listen to their own truths and discover what they are.

Family Rules and Taboos

And then there are the family rules and beliefs about revealing secrets—one of the most taboo arenas in the family psychology. Some of these include

- Don't air the family laundry in public.
- Family business stays behind closed doors.
- Quit blabbing about your personal business.
- Stop that navel gazing—it will only get you in trouble.
- You have quite an imagination!

Traditionally, writers and artists are the "different" ones in the world, the ones who dare challenge the family rules and myths, and even those of society. If you break the family rules, you may feel you aren't accepted or valued, even as you still try to listen to your own voice and keep a connection with the family.

Dealing with Outer and Inner Critics

The way to guard yourself against the assaults of the "outer critics"—whether they are friends, family, or even overzealous writing teachers, is to create a sacred, safe space where you protect your writing from negative or critical feedback. If you don't tell everyone you're writing a memoir, they won't know! If they ask what you are writing about you can give a vague answer. In some cases you may want to tell them you're writing fiction. When people are "too inquisitive," they usually have their own agenda, so be careful how much you reveal.

The combination of the outer critics and the inner critic can be challenging to combat, but if you use boundaries and tools to create safety and separation from those who would interfere, you will find your writing life easier. The inner critic, however, requires some special techniques.

Self-Censorship If you have been shamed, threatened, or shunned by your family for telling the truth, or strongly criticized by teachers or professors about your writing, chances are these experiences have fed into creating a strong inner critic that gets in the way of writing freely.

The inner critic strives to enforce the old rules—stopping us from writing down what we really think or having us pull back from the "real" truth. Over time, we become all too familiar with this negative inner voice.

But if you are to be free to write your truths and your stories, you need to trade in this destructive inner voice for a positive one, and find an antidote to the old negative programs. This may mean more autonomy from the family, or from the old version of family you carry in your mind as you forge a new relationship with yourself.

When my coaching clients tell me about their inner critics, it seems to have an intensity and power on a continuum from extremely negative to seductively soothing. The soothing voice whispers things like, "This is so hard on you. Why don't you just stop; life will be easier. Don't rock the boat."

The inner critic is tenacious. I've never met anyone who didn't have an inner critic, and everyone wants to know how to get rid of it, but the surprising good and bad news is that the critical voice is a part of you. It reflects the natural aspects of being a vulnerable human being with doubts, fears, and worries.

During my Berkeley classes, I ask my students to speak the inner critic's voice into the circle, but the same thing can be achieved by writing down the phrases and answering them. Silence feeds shame. The antidote to this is to state your truth out loud if you are in a group and in your journal as an ongoing exercise in conquering the inner critic.

Ways to Work with the Inner Critic   Write a dialogue with the inner critic. If it says, "You're stupid, you can't write," ask, "Who taught me this? Where did this belief come from?"

If it says, "You're stupid. What makes you think you can write such a long work?" you answer back, "It's true that I didn't know everything, and I was bad in [fill in the blank with school skills], but I have written some good things before, and even [fill in the name of a friend, editor, teacher, family member] liked it."

If you suffered humiliation when you expressed yourself in school or in front of family, write down those phrases. For example, "You always got the worst grade in spelling, and you always failed your essays." Answer back with new phrases that contradict the old voices. "This is not about getting good grades, and I am no longer fourteen years old. I have learned to write well enough, and besides, I can hire an editor if I need to. Just shut up and let me write."

For a few weeks, keep a list of the negative phrases in your head and decide how to counter each with positive, assertive statements. Some of the negative phrases will simply melt away after being acknowledged. See if you can label the origin of the phrase or voice. If the voice says, "Don't you dare tell," respond with, "I'm not telling to embarrass you or to be mean. I just need to tell this story."

If the voice says, "You're going to kill me . . ." you can answer, "You've used guilt to control me for years, but this is my private project, and I must do it. I'm exercising my autonomy now!"

Keep an ongoing list of the critic's attempts to stop you, and keep answering it back. Then get on with your writing for that day.

Balancing the Dark and Light Stories

There is good news about what kinds of stories we need to write. Research has shown that writing our positive stories is as healing as writing our disturbing stories. The technique that I work with in all my coaching and teaching is what I call the "Dark and Light Stories" technique. It is a sandwiching technique that requires us to get clear on what the "light" stories are, and to create lists of both dark and light stories, as we may have done already in the time line and theme exercises.

The Lighter Side

First, make lists of all the lighter stories—those with humor, those about happiness, pleasure, and spirituality—that lift us from the cares and burdens of the world.

Some of these stories include tales of our loved ones, the times when they were there for us, or when people committed acts of kindness or compassion on our behalf. We might think about playing as children, or moments when we felt proud or good about ourselves and our family.

A list of lighter stories might look like this:

- How I learned to ride a bicycle
- The day Mother and I baked cookies
- Grandma's strudel and Grandpa's cigars
- Winning the blue ribbon
- My first car
- Falling in love for the first time
- Our son's birth
- I saw God in the cornfields

It's best to begin writing these positive or uplifting stories to lay a foundation for the other kinds of stories we might need to tell. Keep gathering the lists of the "good" light stories, and put them on your time line. Start writing the positive stories, using scenes and all the details needed to bring them alive for you. Feel the pleasure of the day, the moment, and see and hear all that the story contains. Laugh out loud if it's funny—no one will mind. Immerse yourself in the reality of the happier stories.

Use this list to help you think about topics and themes that remind you of some of the best moments in your life, and then make your own list.

- Peace
- Love
- Vulnerability
- Trust
- Joy
- Awe
- Generosity
- Selflessness
- Serenity
- Courage
- Radiance
- Nature
- Admiration

The Darker Side

As you approach the darker stories, do it with caution and respect for the tenderness and vulnerability you might feel. First make a list of the stories that you know are the darker ones, and allow room for stories that may still be murky, but you suspect are at the edges of your memory. Try to identify the themes of the stories. Include them on your time line, or you can just put the list away for awhile.

Darker Themes

- Pain
- Despair
- Vulnerability

- Fear
- Jealousy
- Longing
- Abuse
- Rejection
- Despair
- Depression
- Death
- Loss
- Illness

For your writing process, create a light-dark-light "sandwich" of stories. Start with several positive stories to build the foundations we have discussed, then write one of the darker stories, and immediately after choose one of the lighter themes or a story from your time line and write it. Balancing your writing sessions between the dark and the light stories helps to maintain an emotional balance that you can draw on for the long term.

Harry Potter's Technique

Sometimes our writing takes us past our barred gates and un-welcome memories come rushing out. How can we cope with this? How do we face unwanted truths?

Recently, as I watched the Harry Potter movie *The Prisoner of Azkaban*, I noticed a technique that helped Harry confront terror. The professor told him to hold in his mind the best memory of his life at the same time as he cast a spell on a terrifying apparition that represented his deepest fears. If the positive image was not strong enough, the spell would not work.

The first time Harry tried, terror overcame him and the professor had to put the apparition, the "dementor," back into the closet. He had Harry focus more, holding the image of his best memory even more clearly. He stood taller, he took a deep breath, and held his image carefully while the apparition was released. Harry vanquished it with a flick of his wand and a spellbreaker word. The professor asked him what he was thinking. "I thought of my parents." Harry was an orphaned child, but he held in his heart the powerful love he knew they felt for him, and that love vanquished his worst fears.

I suggest a similar technique to all memoir writers, though we must make do without the magic wand! Hold the images of the positive, light stories—the ones that fill you with joy, love, or peace—in your body and mind along with some positive phrases such as, "I need to free my voice" or "I give myself permission to write my truth." Then, as you write the darker stories, limit how long you labor over the story. Write for shorter periods, fifteen to twenty minutes, and then switch to a lighter story. You can return to the darker story until you finish it, but the idea is to contain the darkness and expand the positive feelings into a foundation from which to work from now on.

Writing Exercises

1. Write a story your family would call false, a lie, or not true.
2. Write a story your family would call true, but that you think is false.
3. Write a scene about your family that shows its philosophy about life: "we are very close," "we are not religious," "we are not prejudiced," and so forth.
4. What family secret(s) are you supposed to keep? Make a list.
5. Write a story you thought you would never be able to write.
6. Inner critic: List all the nasty things your inner critic says as a matter of habit.

7. Dark and light: Keep separate lists of the dark stories and the light stories, and continue to note the theme and where they fit on the time line.

8. Write about the happiest day of your life.

Now that you have the raw material and several story topics and themes gathered for your memoir, we will look at how to assemble them into a workable manuscript by examining story structure, the arc of narrative story writing, and the tools needed to make your stories come together into a finished work.

STEP 6

Organizing the Narrative Arc

Two or three things I know for sure, and one of them is that to go on living, I have to tell stories, that stories are the one sure thing I know to touch the heart and change the world.
—*Dorothy Allison*

Most memoir writers' eyes begin to glaze over and they fidget in their seats when I talk about story structure and the narrative arc in my workshops. Sighing, they say, "What do you mean by narrative arc? I want to use my diary and journals for my memoir. Do I have to learn all this technical stuff?"

The answer is YES! The more you develop the craft of writing a story and learn about classical narrative forms, the more choices you will have as you create your memoir.

Why Does Your Memoir Need Dramatic Structure?

At the heart of a well-told story is dramatic structure. When you read a story with suspense and conflict, you keep asking, "What happens next?" Though as readers we may be unaware of it, we bring innate expectations about what we want to happen in a story. We express our satisfaction and pleasure in a story well told when we put down a book and say, "That was a great story. It kept my attention all the way through."

The need to understand more about ourselves and the human condition through story is a need that resides deep in the human psyche. Storytelling has been around for millennia, and through stories we expand our capacity to connect with the experiences of our fellow travelers on the planet and learn more about ourselves.

According to John Gardner, author of *The Art of Fiction*, the world within a story needs to be created seamlessly so that it can work its magic upon us. "Fiction does its work by creating a dream in the reader's mind."

This statement remains true for memoir writers as well. The demands of storytelling make it imperative to shape our stories so that our readers can inhabit the seamless structure of our narrative. Think about books you have read, whether fiction or nonfiction. If you stopped reading, do you know why? The story failed in ways that can be analyzed and corrected. For instance, in the contests and submissions I read, the pieces that don't work for me are those where I discover some kind of flaw in the structure—there is no clear entry into the story, it's riddled with confusing flashbacks, then leaps back and forth in time, it's repetitive, there's no beginning, middle, or end—these are all problems that cause the narrative to lose its power to keep me in the "dream."

It can be challenging to learn new techniques, but it's important to learn more about structure, scenes, and fictional tools such as point of view, dialogue, and shaping of a piece with conflict and action. As you learn these techniques, you might be surprised at how many insights you discover from translating your memories into story form and creating a work that is satisfying for your readers.

The Importance of Choosing Your Scenes and Turning Points

Because we experience life chronologically, without a clear beginning, middle, or end, memoirists tend to write in an episodic way—"this happened, then that happened, and after that . . ."—and are often overwhelmed by a huge array of memories and details. When deluged by details and feelings, it's difficult to sort out what to include, how to create a plot, and how to see friends and family as "characters."

But the transition from "all these things happened to me" to choosing and shaping your narrative using the tools of fiction must happen in order for your writing to lift out of a journaling form into story and narrative. And as you work to create a form and shape to your story, choosing your turning points and finding your conflicts, characters, plot, and narrative arc, you are changed by this process. Elizabeth Lyon discusses how stories are transformational in her book A *Writer's Guide to Fiction:* "Told artfully, a story can move you and alter your brain chemistry. By knowing my story . . . you might be transformed." In Step Eight, we will examine the research and the ways that writing is healing, but for now let's examine the rules of story and how to create what is called the "narrative arc."

Story Structure and the Narrative Arc

Here are some important things to remember when creative your narrative arc.

- Unlike journaling, a story has a form—a beginning, middle, and an end. Another way to think about this is that your story, your book, needs to have a dramatic structure: Act One, Act Two, and Act Three.
- Something significant happens in each scene of the story—this is the point of the scene.

- A story has a reason for being told—this is your theme.
- The main character, the protagonist—in a memoir it's you!—is changed significantly by events, actions, decisions, and epiphanies. The growth and change of the main character is imperative in any story, and is the primary reason a memoir is written—to show the arc of character change from beginning to end.
- All stories have conflict, rising action, a crisis, a climax, and a resolution.
- By the end, the story world, the world where the protagonist began, is transformed.

Some memoirists begin with a prologue that establishes the author's voice and intent before getting into the main story—the beginning, middle, and end. It's important to note that standard dramatic story structure has been around since Aristotle's time; it's a classic form that reaches into the psychology of human beings and offers a universal message.

Focusing Your Theme in the Arc

As you plan your story, clarify your themes. Being certain about them will help you build your book toward the final resolution of the theme's questions and conflicts by the end of the narrative arc, the end of the book.

Many memoirists explore how certain events changed their lives irrevocably, such as Alice Sebold in *Lucky*, the story of a rape, or Augusten Burroughs in *Running with Scissors*, the tale of surviving a bizarre and chaotic childhood. Another theme is recovering from the death of a loved one—such as *The Year of Magical Thinking* by Joan Didion, or *Paula* by Isabel Allende.

Patricia Hampl's *The Florist's Daughter* or Mary Gordon's *Circling My Mother* shows the heartbreak and challenging difficulties of aging and dying parents. Sexual abuse is explored in Kathryn Harrison's

The Kiss, and mental illness is the topic of Susan Kaysen's *Girl, Interrupted* and *An Unquiet Mind* by Kay Jamison. There are countless varieties of themes, but though books may have the same theme, the stories, language, and structure make each book unique. It's imperative that you develop your skills to allow your story to shine.

To clarify your choice of theme for your narrative arc, ask the following questions:

- What is the main, dominant meaning of my story?
- What is my book about? (One sentence.)
- How does my book end? What do I want the reader to understand and learn?

Three Acts of Dramatic Structure

Act One (Beginning)

The first act sets up the story, introducing the characters and situations that show conflicting desires and complications through different scenes. During this act you present the context: the who, what, when, where, and why of the story.

Act Two (Middle)

Drawing upon scenes and summaries, the story action rises through conflicts, complications, and challenges that the protagonist keeps attempting to solve. As the story progresses, even more complications develop that thwart an easy or quick resolution.

Act Three (End)

In the last act, the protagonist wrestles with the forces that have been working against her; this is shown through what is called the crisis and the climax of the story. Then follows the denouement or epiphany that resolves the loose ends of the story. The crisis may be thought of as a spiritual challenge or a dark night of the soul where the deepest beliefs and core truths of the character are tested. The climax is the highest level of tension and conflict that the protagonist must resolve as the story comes to a close.

Let's examine a classic memoir written by the now famous author Tobias Wolff to study how he developed his story through the three-act structure.

This Boy's Life by Tobias Wolff
Act One

In *This Boy's Life*, written in 1989, we are introduced to the young Tobias with this first line:

Our car boiled over again just after my mother and I crossed the Continental Divide.

Here, in the first words of the memoir, we experience a tone of warning. A few moments later, we see a nearby truck crash over a cliff, and the mother's anxious looks at her son, as if appreciating the fact that he was alive and with her.

Next, we are given a clue to character of young Toby: *I saw that the time was right to make a play for souvenirs. I knew she had no money for them . . . but now that her guard was down, I couldn't help myself.* We see him as self-aware, wily, and manipulative, and a scathingly honest narrator.

The theme of the book is introduced in this way: *It was 1955, and we were driving from Florida to Utah to get away from a man my mother was afraid of and to get rich on uranium. We were going to change our luck.*

With such an introduction, we already know that no one is going to get rich, that there is more to fear, and their luck will not change.

We learn about the fractured relationship between his mother and father, and the fact that the family has been split down the middle: Tobias goes with his mother, who has no money, and the father refuses to pay support to Tobias and his mother. But his brother lives with the well-off father and goes to prep school—a very different kind of life. Despite, or perhaps because of his confessional tone, we're sympathetic to the main character, already informed that things are going to go awry—and we want to know how this will happen—which creates suspense.

In this opening act, we have the who, what, when, where, and why of the story, and we are launched into the adventure of finding out more about these characters. We want to know what will happen that might change their luck, and what new trouble they will find. We can feel it coming.

Act Two

In Act Two, trouble has fully arrived and life has become more complex emotionally for everyone, especially the narrator. There's a sharp divide between the narrator's outer life and his inner struggles, and a buildup of several factors that need resolution: his increasingly dangerous and delinquent behavior; the violent, but occasionally intimate relationship with Dwight, the man who becomes his stepfather; and the affectionate, protective relationship Toby has with his mother. As the middle portion of the book develops, violence and danger occur more frequently, seen through many short precise scenes that keep us reading and eager to find out how and if the conflicts will be resolved. We watch young Toby, called Jack in the book, plunge further into his identity conflict and get into more troubles with duplicity, lies, and out-of-control delinquent behavior. He endures cruel treatment and beatings from his stepfather, and these become even more brutal. By being privy to Toby's carefully selected thoughts, desires, and fantasy world, we understand him deeply, and see how little he's able to protect himself or his mother, whom he loves above all else, but who's caught in the same trap with him. He sees that he's unable to save herself or himself from the dismal life they've fallen into once she marries Dwight.

Act Three

By the time we get to Act Three, we are driven to find out what happens, to find out if there is a resolution of the complications of the first two acts. We are still rooting for the narrator to see his way through to a new and different life he has been imagining, something other than living a half-life in a town where everyone is a loser. A major turning point occurs when Toby commits fraud to get admitted into prep school. This daring act, still a relic of his delinquent yet hopeful self, helps him to escape his prison, and gives his mother the courage to leave the abusive husband. Despite some recurring loose ends at the end of the book, we see the threads of hope for his life. Because he's Tobias Wolff, we know that somehow he makes it all the way to the best-seller list, which adds a dose of irony to the experience of reading his memoir. Neither the Toby of the story nor today's reader would ever guess that outcome from this coming-of-age memoir.

Suspense and Mystery in Stories

At the heart of every story is a mystery. We want to know how the narrator coped with the challenging events and conflicts presented in Act One. When reading *A Hole in the World* we see young Richard Rhodes finding his way to freedom from terrible loss and a frightening stepmother. Even if we know that he becomes a famous man, we keep turning the pages so we can find out *how* he escapes and *how* he heals the abuse he suffered. In *Paula*, we want to know what helps Isabel Allende make sense of the death of her daughter, knowing that the act of telling her daughter the family stories is an act of healing.

Through powerful scenes showing specific life-changing events, we learn about how families deal with immigration and identity issues in books like *Catfish and Mandela* or *The Unwanted*. There are the challenges and delights of the spiritual journey in *Cloister Walk* by Kathleen Norris, or in Anne Lamott's books on spirituality, or in Karen Armstrong's *The Spiral Staircase*. Class and sexual prejudice are explored in *Two or Three Things I Know for Sure* by Dorothy Allison or *All Souls: A Family Story from Southie* by Michael Macdonald.

In *The Glass Castle* by Jeannette Walls, the family chaos accelerates throughout the narrator's childhood with no major "aha" moment or resolution. But by the end, the narrator is free to live her own life and sees her unconventional parents through the eyes of her adult compassionate self.

Where Does Your Story End?

In planning your themes and the narrative arc, it's important to get an idea of how your story ends. That's why many writers find it very important and helpful to make an outline, whether or not you know how you will get from X to Y; and remember, it's not carved in stone. An outline allows us to get some perspective on the chaos of "real life" and to impose the shape of a story.

Knowing the end will help you visualize the beginning and the middle. As T. S. Eliot famously said in his *Four Quartets*:

The end is where we start from.

If you are not clear about the way your book will end, then decide what the crisis or the climax might be—a moment of greatest change or insight, when your life and your understanding of yourself shifted irrevocably. After that comes the denouement that ties together the end pieces of the story.

Building Blocks of the Narrative Arc

Each chapter in the book and the scenes that make up each chapter are building blocks of the story that can be planned in your outline. Now that we have the overview, let's look at the particular ways that structure is built scene by scene, and assembled into chapters that become beads on the string of the narrative arc of your story.

Scenes and Chapters

After you have sorted through the memories and moments of your story, you need to

- Note where the major turning points occur on the time line
- Define the theme that each vignette or chapter addresses
- Use scenes to show significant action

Scenes are building blocks of a narrative that show the action as if on the stage. These moments of "being there," where the reader is brought into the story world, are created through the use of sensual details, dialogue, and description. Remember the old cliché: "show, don't tell." As we experience the world of the scene, our senses are engaged.

Each scene shows

- Some significant event or challenge that advances the action
- A protagonist with ongoing conflicts and problems that are not immediately solvable
- A setting where the action takes place
- A time frame for the action

Characters are developed in each scene, preferably through dialogue and action. Be sure to include sensual details such as sight, sound, smell, and feeling. Use colors, texture, and smell to enhance a scene. Strong verbs and nouns enhance the feeling of being in the world of the story.

List of Scene Elements

Each time you write a scene, be sure to check these elements of how you build a scene.

1. Place, setting: Include landscape, weather, buildings, towns, cities, roads, and houses. Describe carefully and with sensual detail the colors, sounds, and feeling of your story's setting.

2. Characters: through dialogue and action, your characters will reveal themselves.
   - Rather than *tell* us someone's philosophy of life, *show* how that character lives it.
   - Telling: *"He was generous, confident, and likable."*
   - Showing: *"He threw down a five-dollar bill for the cup of coffee, winked at the waitress, and walked out, his coattails swinging."*

3. Situation: What's the situation or problem? Good storytelling means there's a point to the scene, or a conflict that needs resolution. It can be subtle, such as the desire for an ice cream cone, or emotionally quite large—such as the abandonment or abuse of a child.

4. Action: How people react and respond directs the forward movement and action of the story. Action furthers the plot. Action—we don't mean car chases here—moves the story into the next paragraph and chapter, and leads to the development of plot. People make choices, and these choices show character and create the next event that characters react to. Even reflection can be a subtle action, as decisions arise from it.

5. Dialogue: Style of conversation and turns of phrase help define character, making a scene play out on the page

moment by moment. Dialogue is not necessary for every scene, but too often memoir writers narrate almost everything, without using enough dialogue to bring the scene and characters to life. Writing dialogue takes practice, so begin today!

- When you need to indicate which character spoke the dialogue, it's best to use the conventional verb "said": *"Please, please, don't go. I'll do anything . . . ," he said.*
- Other verbs, such as "pleaded" or "whined" or "screamed," detract from the dialogue, and are a form of *telling* readers how the characters feel; let the characters' words *show* their emotion.
- Too much direct dialogue can cause time in a scene to slow down. Too much back-and-forth dialogue without sensual details feels like watching a tennis match.
- For variety, use indirect dialogue: *She told me she was going to leave me. She said she never wanted to see me again, and sat back in her seat, sipping her tea.*

6. When does the story occur in time? Research can help you give clues to the time frame in which the story takes place. Think of details such as transportation, music, clothes, and social etiquette.

7. Sensual details help us to know how the story world feels, smells, tastes, and sounds. Description is a tool that helps the reader feel and sense the scene, involving him emotionally. The reader needs to *see* the place and the action; *hear* the sound of the environment—nature, wind, cars, animals, or people talking—and *experience* the feel of clothes on skin, the humidity, the sun, or the dampness of fog. Description is a vivid portrayal that shows a world in its full experiential glory. We may use metaphor and similes, vivid details of color, sound, smell, and a sensory experience of touch and texture.

Just as a painting has shades of color, so does a descriptive passage in your writing. Moods are portrayed through use of color and contrast. For instance, a rainy day is grey, there's a bluish cast on faces, and a reflection on the sidewalk. A sunny day in the same location is different, with shadows and complementary colors—purple shadows against yellow flowers. You may envision your character's mood as similar to the weather or the dingy location, or contrasting them. Such details add clarity and specificity to your writing.

Setting and context ground a scene in the real world. Add characters, conflict, action, and dialogue, and you have a story. We enter the world of characters, seeing the world revealed through their eyes. We are transported to John Gardner's previously mentioned dream world of language.

Here's an example of a partial scene from *The Glass Castle* by Jeannette Walls. Jeannette and her family were hungry all the time, and often the refrigerator was empty. Notice the specifics in this scene, and the sensual details.

Dad . . . came home with a bag of groceries: a can of corn, a half gallon of milk, a loaf of bread, two tins of deviled ham, a sack of sugar, and a stick of margarine. . . . I found Lori in the kitchen eating something out of a cup with a spoon. I looked in the refrigerator. There was nothing inside but a half-gone stick of margarine.

"Lori, what are you eating?"

"Margarine," she said.

I wrinkled my nose. "Really?"

"Yeah," she said. "Mix it with sugar. Tastes just like frosting."

I made some. It didn't taste like frosting. It was sort of crunchy, because the sugar didn't dissolve, and it was greasy and left a filmy coat in my mouth.

The scene shows what is happening so we can see and feel it. We taste the greasy margarine, we feel the desperate hunger, and we want to know how these people will find a way to change their hopeless situation.

Emotion in Memoir Writing

A challenging problem for memoir writers is how much emotion to show, and to have a sense of how much is implied in the story, especially if it's a very emotional story. If you as the narrator present a surplus of emotion on the page, your reader may have trouble sorting out the feelings. When it comes to emotional detail, "Less is more." Containment allows readers to imagine the feelings being described, and gives them room for their own feelings to come forward. Your job is to create the scenes where the characters are experiencing emotion, and show enough for the reader to understand and empathize. Such terms as "screamed, shrieked, exploded" for instance, can be too melodramatic. Describing a situation and showing it with thoughts and actions that guide readers allows them to inhabit the situation and feel what *they* feel, not only what you felt. The reader does not want to be manipulated by the writer about exactly how to feel, so it's your job to create a situation—through language, tone, and phrase—that creates emotion in your reader. Read poetry or fine literature for examples of writing that shows emotion with balance, drama, and power. Look at the works listed in the recommended reading list, for instance, the different styles of Virginia Woolf, F. Scott Fitzgerald, and Toni Morrison. And be sure to read all kinds of poetry and attend poetry readings to learn about metaphor, precise language, and creating emotion through imagery and tone.

In this passage by Virginia Woolf from *A Sketch of the Past*, she's reflecting on the suicide of a friend. Note the way she uses nature and metaphor to show her feelings.

*I remember . . . walking on the path by the apple tree. It seemed
to me that the apple tree was connected with the horror of Mr.
Valpy's suicide . . . I stood there looking at the grey-green
creases of the bark—it was a moonlit night—in a trance of
horror. I seemed to be dragged down, hopelessly, into some pit of
absolute despair from which I could not escape.*

Reflection

In *This Boy's Life*, Tobias Wolff interweaves his adult perceptions
about the childhood experiences he's describing. This comes from
the section of the book where Tobias forges the papers to apply to
the prep school:

*I was writing the truth. It was truth known only to me, but I
believed in it more than I believed in the facts arrayed against it. I
believed . . . I was a straight A student . . . an Eagle Scout
. . . a boy of integrity. These were ideas about myself that I had
held on to for dear life. Now I gave them voice.*

In this reflection, the older narrator is aware of what the boy was
not—what he believed about himself against all odds, showing the
passion he has to become that person. In several places in the book,
Wolff enters the story as the adult narrator, whereas most of the
time the child narrator's voice is the one we hear. When the adult
comes in, he adds a layer of understanding and tension, because the
reader does not know how the young rebel became the Tobias
Wolff we know today.

Alternate Structures

Though it is important to keep in mind the continuing engaging
action of the narrative arc, there are many different ways to
accomplish that goal. Once you have a sense of where the story

is going, you can choose different points of view and structural options that can present the story in interesting ways.

Different Narrators

Some books are "I" narratives with a single point of view. Some books have different narrators to tell the story, such as *The Color of Water* by James McBride. A Jewish woman narrates the first chapter, the next chapter is in McBride's voice, and throughout the book both voices weave the story. In *Brother I'm Dying*, Edwidge Danticat interweaves her story with that of her father and his brother by using different points of view. In her own narrative, she is the witness in various scenes, but in other chapters, she narrates family stories and history.

Too many points of view can become disjointed and confusing, so be careful to select and link the voices in a consistent manner that will preserve the integrity and coherence of the narrative.

Entering and Flashing Back

One classic book structure that I've seen frequently in memoir writing is to start at a particularly significant, climactic moment or turning point in your story and then flash back to the beginning. Where you start is extremely important, because people tend to stop reading a story if it doesn't grab their attention right away. Many fine writers select a great moment to start with a bang, and then go back to the beginning to choose other scenes that led up to it.

As these examples show, the form of a book can take any of a number of shapes and paths, but the writer needs to fully understand the "rules" of story. If you want to use a less traditional approach, make sure each narrative thread has its own arc with conflicts, crisis, climax, and resolution.

Frame Structures

The frame structure used in novels and memoirs is a device that organizes and allows movement between different time frames. A "frame" structure is like bookends, with the beginning and the end written in one time frame, and the middle in another. There are various ways to work with the frame structure, such as using past and present tenses to help convey where the story is in time, keeping the tenses consistent within each part of the frame structure.

In the frame structure, the narrator can begin in the "now" of current time to offer a voice that can contain and give a perspective on another part of the frame—a story set in the past—and then return to the present at the other end.

Sometimes past and present time weaves back and forth between chapters, or you can use a circular construction that weaves through time, location, and point of view. An example of an alternative form of memoir is Maxine Hong Kingston's *The Woman Warrior: Memoirs of a Girlhood Among Ghosts*. There's debate about whether or not this book, based on oral family stories and Maxine's own immigrant experience, is fiction or memoir. Imagination, nonlinear stories, and several points of view make the case for fiction, but Maxine calls it a memoir because it's based on her family's stories and her cultural tradition of storytelling.

Another memoir, Amos Oz's *A Tale of Love and Darkness*, is told in a nonlinear way through different points of view, using imagination and speculation about past events he didn't witness, traversing backwards and forward through time into the nineteenth century, telling the story of war, the formation of Israel, the history of a family, and his own struggles.

Reading many different memoirs and taking note of the structure will help you to get a feel for how structure and style help to determine the tone and feeling of a memoir.

Writing Exercises

1. Draw upon your turning points and time line to create the significant events in Act One. Make a list, and think about how these events build conflict and suspense.

2. For Act Two, list the major conflicts, significant moments, and big events over time, with an eye to how they might be resolved in Act Three.

3. For Act Three, consider your moments of deepest crisis when you were most tested, and what you did to resolve those challenges. Make a list and keep writing in journal fashion if you are not sure what or where the crisis or climax will be.

4. Practice writing scenes. Use the checklist of scene elements to help you develop them.

5. Choose scenes from your favorite memoir or fiction and write out or type up some of it to get the feeling of what it's like to write a scene. This is for practice so your body can get the feel of word rhythms and a sense of how a scene builds.

6. Focus on writing scenes for your most significant turning points, making sure that each scene has an arc of action and character development.

7. Select some memoirs to read from the list and note the structure. Read them at first for the overview, but see if you can catch the turning points, and how the crisis and climax develops. This will be different for each book.

8. Outline the structure of a book you like. See if you can notice where the three acts begin and end. In a finished book, this is made seamless, so it operates mostly in your subconscious.

Writing and Rewriting—On Your Way to the Final Manuscript

Finding your structure is one of the most important things you can do to organize and make sense of the multitude of details that are part of your "real" life and memories. Once you have solved your structural problems, you'll find that finishing your book becomes simpler and easier. As you work through the drafts, you're engaged in a process of writing, visioning, revisioning—which means "seeing again"—and rewriting. Allow yourself to enjoy rewriting—it's at least two-thirds of the writing process. All good writers go through a process of rewriting many drafts. As John Updike said, "Writing and rewriting are a constant search for what one is saying."

Once you have a draft that pleases you, you're ready to edit—and to decide if, or how, you want to publish your work. Some writers don't feel a desire to publish their memoir, especially if it was for the purpose of self-growth and healing, but others feel moved to share it in the spirit of helping people benefit and learn from their experiences.

In the next chapter, Step Seven, we'll explore the issue of ethics in publishing a memoir, and how to publish through the various means available in the current marketplace.

STEP 7

To Publish—or Not

If there's a book you really want to read but it hasn't been written yet, then you must write it.

—*Toni Morrison*

After many months, perhaps years, of writing and gathering stories, the time has finally come when you need to make a decision: shall I publish my memoir—or not?

Many factors come into play when it's time to make this important decision. Some of the most important are the ethical issues that arise when thinking about sharing an intensely personal and private work. Unlike fiction writers, memoirists aren't able to hide behind what I call "the fictional wall"—unless of course they decide to alter the life stories they've written and publish them as fiction.

When publishing a memoir, there's an implied contract with the reader that they are reading *nonfiction*, that all the major characters and scenes are based on truth, that memories and the chaos of life events have been shaped into a story with major events presented as accurately as possible. Recently, readers have been disappointed and offended when they've learned that some very popular best-selling memoirs were substantially fictional.

In this chapter we'll consider the ethical questions that arise for most memoirists, then look at publishing options.

Ethical Issues Memoir Writers Struggle With

Every day Google sends me a link to articles about memoir writing. Some connect me to current books, and others tell me about discussions at conferences and in blogs about the intersection between publishing and memoir writing.

Two Types of Concerns

Memoirists who decide to publish seem to gather into two general camps:

1. The in-your-face, devil-may-care writer who's casual or even cocky about what he or she has exposed in the memoir. This type is not worried about negative reactions by family, friends, or the larger public, even reveling in revealing juicy secrets and personal details that other people save for best friends or therapists. Perhaps laced with a bit of exhibitionism, these writers are entertaining on panel discussions or book tours. The more fuss and controversy, the better.

2. The other kind of writer shyly peeks out from behind her desk, which is lined with family pictures, saying, "I just had to publish this but I hope no one minds. Please don't get mad at me—I'm simply writing my truth. I mean no harm."

This second kind of memoirist is the one I most often meet in workshops and classes, a person who's concerned about personal relationships and wants to preserve them while also following her desire to put her writing into the public eye. She's unsure about how to approach family and friends, and has panic attacks at night about how much she's revealed. She needs to think about the choices she has for getting her work published while learning how to manage the conflicts she feels regarding revealing her life in public. The following section is geared toward her and other memoirists like her.

Common Concerns

These are the kinds of concerns that may arise:

- I can't publish these stories—what if it hurts the feelings of people I care about?
- Should I worry about being sued for writing the truth?
- I have a right to do whatever I want with my truth—don't I?
- Do I have to talk to my family about what I've written? What should I say?
- If my family tells me not to publish my story, do I have to obey them?
- How do I decide what to include? I want to tell my truths and be honest, but I don't want to hurt anyone.

Another student told me, "My sister said she'd pay me never to write my story." Someone at a conference raised her hand and confessed, "I've been forbidden to publish my story. I love my family, but I really want to get my story into the world. I feel it can help other women who've been abused." After her confession, a lively discussion went on for another twenty minutes as other writers brought up their own dilemmas about how much to reveal, how to protect family members and yet tell their own truths, and whether they should wait until people die before publishing.

Of course, each person must make decisions based on his or her own particular story, family, and ethics, but the challenge of an ethical decision tugs at them. It can be a very emotional time. You need to assess where you feel you can take a stand about your story and the personal information in it, and how much you feel it will hurt or help any of the relationships in your life.

Do No Harm

Dr. James Pennebaker, the major researcher on writing as healing whom you will read more about in Step Eight, says that the first version of your story invites you to tunnel into the layers of your life and yourself. But when it comes to publishing, he urges caution. "Secrets are part of society's protective mechanism. My motto is, 'Do no harm.'"

The fabric of our emotional, familial, and even societal lives is made of circles of intimacy. On the outer ring are people we don't know, with concentric layers representing those with whom we are more intimate. The people in the innermost circle are likely to be familiar with most of your stories, having witnessed or lived through them with you. People in the outer rings of intimacy may not know the more personal stories. With each person we reveal different aspects of who we are.

One of my students said, "I don't mind if strangers know my secrets, but my colleagues and friends . . . that's a different story."

Think about your inner and outer circles, and assess the revealing material in your book before proceeding to talk to family and friends.

We've already discussed how family members recall events differently, having maintained an uneasy truce about certain issues only to have it break down when someone—you—decide to write a memoir. Then, the tension really rises when you talk with them about publishing it.

Imagine strangers or friends reading the intimate details in your story. As you review each story or chapter, consider what the risks of publication might be. If you feel your story is too personal to make public or that doing so would make you too vulnerable, are you prepared to let it go? It's all right not to do anything with your writing beside enjoying the satisfaction of having gone through an important process of healing, sorting, and finding a new perspective. Enjoy the results of your work, and put it aside. Later on, you might open that drawer and reconsider what you want to do with it.

On Writing the Truth About Loved Ones

One of my students, Denise Roessle, wrote this about her process of writing and publishing.

> I'm constantly wrestling with how much truth to reveal about family and friends who are still alive. During my pregnancy I lived with a woman who had an enormous heart and a huge drinking problem. I witnessed a lot over those seven months, and while it's not all relevant to my story, some of it is. We became friends and still are, 32 years later. I worry that portraying her honestly will hurt her, and I find myself going back over that part of the story, looking for ways to soften it without totally sacrificing the truth.
>
> With my parents, who played a major role in what happened, it's even worse. A little voice in my head says: "These people aren't monsters. It couldn't have been that bad. They love you, and what you're doing is going to kill them." I envision them completely cutting me off once the book is out, and my sister and brother being angry with me for spilling my guts in public. Sometimes I catch myself wishing that they were already dead so I wouldn't have to worry about their reaction.
>
> I don't want to hurt anybody, but I need to tell my story, to say the truth and be heard. For once, I'm making my needs more important than everyone else's. I'm going ahead with it, letting the chips fall where they may. That decision alone has been a major step toward healing.

Some writers insist that telling the truth openly is one of the things they really need to do. When people grow up in a house full of secrets, part of the healing process is to break out of the darkness and trap of so many secrets and rules about not telling anyone about what is true and real.

You need to assess what is best for you. Many authors have had to wrestle with the reactions of family after being published.

Blackbird and *Still Waters*, memoirs by Jennifer Lauck, were published to great critical acclaim. Lauck is the only remaining member of her original family. In *Blackbird*, the narrator is a seven-year-old child who presents her feelings about complex living arrangements and decisions that profoundly affect her life. She's very young when her mother dies, and her father remarries soon after. *Still Waters* continues her story into adolescence and adulthood, as she revisits childhood mysteries and fills in other layers of the story.

After publication of *Blackbird*, Lauck found herself embroiled in a disagreement with her stepmother and stepsiblings, who accused her of lying and presenting incidents that made them look bad. When and under what circumstances the relationship between Lauck's father and stepmother developed is one of the matters disputed by the stepfamily.

A few years after publication of both memoirs, Salon.com published an article about their family conflict, a kind of cautionary tale. In it, Lauck defended her work, saying, ". . . this is the memory of a little girl, and I wrote it to the best of my ability, and I stand behind it 100 percent."

True or False

It's understood that no one can "prove" or justify memories. Through the years we've seen stories about families torn asunder by painful accusations made as a result of "recovered" memories. The person making the accusation asserts that a memory of abuse by a family member, usually the father, was repressed for years but then recovered during the process of therapy, sometimes under hypnosis. She wants legal justice, but the judicial system doesn't usually send people to jail without a witness to the crime. According to the law, a memory is not an objective fact.

As a therapist, I've seen how memories can suddenly appear in the therapy hour, and cause great psychic trauma for the client. What the client does about it becomes part of the therapy. Whether the memory is "true" or not isn't our focus; instead, we work on how to heal the wounds that are now part of the person's conscious experience.

There have been several incidents where "recovered memories" have been famously recanted and disavowed, sometimes long after accusations of abuse have destroyed a family. Fathers or other family members have gone to jail for many years based on testimony—by witnesses who also have "recovered memories" of their sister, daughter, or niece's abuse—that turns out not to be true. But when this occurs, there is usually either an underlying emotional problem that still needs resolution, or a residue of guilt and shame over the false memory that also needs healing.

A Useful Disclaimer

Because of the controversy about memory, it's become standard at the beginning of memoirs to present a statement that goes something like this:

> *This is my story, and I've told it as I remember it to the best of my ability. I know that everyone does not see the world through my eyes, but I've done my best to write the truth as I see it. I can't decide what is true for others. My intent is to share the story that I know, and I invite those who disagree with me to write their own.*

If there are situations, characters, or events that have been altered for the purpose of brevity, to protect the innocent or the guilty, or to create a workable story, the author may say:

> *The names of people in my memoir have been changed for their protection, and I've blended some scenes and events and short-ened others to protect their identity. The names of locations have been changed, but if you are from my hometown, you'll recognize the landmarks. I stand behind the truth of the events and memories, and hope that if I've made any mistakes, they will be forgiven.*

Tips for Making Ethical Decisions About Your Memoir

If you're writing about events and situations that you assume will elicit shame or guilt, it's important for your own healing that you complete the writing before deciding to confront family members with it. The same is true if you are still angry about what happened. Write your story until you have burned off the largest ridges of guilt, grudges, and revenge. You'll end up with a more resolved and healed version of your story. Time and layers of writing help this to happen. Then ask yourself this:

- Are there serious grudges or emotional cutoffs between you and family and friends? If so, try to find ways to bridge the gaps before you publish your memoir.
- Do you want to *ask permission* or do you want to *tell* your family what you are writing about?
- "Asking permission" means the request can be denied, which will affect your topics and how you write about them. Be clear before you speak about your intentions or make requests to others.

- Be prepared to negotiate sticky issues when you bring up the person's appearance in a memoir.

Checklist

- If you use real names, get permission. After you write your piece, show it to the people named and obtain their written consent before putting it in print.
- If your piece reveals information about a town, public figures, or events, be sure that your facts are accurate.
- Make certain that you are not defaming anyone's character or invading their privacy. Check with a literary attorney to find out what these terms mean. If you have a publisher, the staff and attorneys will work with you on this, but if you publish independently, you need to take care of it yourself.
- As you do your research, check as many facts as possible for situations that are about recordable and public events. Even then, people's memories may not be in agreement.
- If people other than family members are included in the book, be willing to change names, physical descriptions, and the locations of towns or other public places.
- Fictionalizing, or changing certain things to protect the guilty and the innocent, may be necessary when preparing for publication. It might be a good idea to say in your introduction that changes were made in the literal truth of the story.

Preparing to Publish Your Memoir

Today's publishing marketplace includes an enormous range of print and digital print-on-demand publishing opportunities, from the traditional commercial route to Lulu, iUniverse, Amazon Book Surge, e-zines and literary journals, Web sites, and blogs—either your own or those where you can post your stories for an audience of subscribers.

The choices can seem overwhelming, but it's all great news! The days of there being only way to get your work into the world— a large publisher in New York—are over. There are so many choices now and new direct ways to reach potential readers. Learning about the wonderful variety of choices available to you only empowers you to make the best selection for your book and your goals.

Reconsidering Your Narrative Voice

As you approach your later drafts, you'll begin to experience your story on a new level, viewing it finally as a "manuscript." Each editing pass you make brings your work into focus as a story, leaving behind your "real life" memories. At this point you will want to reread your story with an ear for your narrator's voice.

What kind of tone and attitude is conveyed by your narrator throughout the book?

Does he or she sound humorous, angry, resentful?

If the narrator conveys a judgmental or angry attitude, the reader may feel manipulated to feel exactly as the narrator does, but the story is best conveyed with enough balanced distance for readers to draw their own conclusions. Presenting the story in scenes and with sensual details to convey the narrator's world in its fullest context will help your story be embraced by a wider audience. Remember too that your duty as an author is to present the world of the characters without manipulating the reader into feeling specific reactions. We discussed this in the section on emotion in memoir writing, Step Six. Writing and rewriting many times will help you to find the proper balance between your own feelings and the story you want to tell. Your early drafts may be rants, but your later drafts should not be.

Improving Characterization

Are any of your characters drawn with all good or all bad traits? Are they subtle, nuanced real people, or two-dimensional characters, like clichés in a comic book?

Even if, for the sake of truth, you must show the "real" people in your life as "dark" characters, most people have some number of positive human traits. However, balancing positive and negative traits can be a problem if the story is about abuse, tragedies of war, or other situations where very dark deeds or cruelty are portrayed.

If the author has worked out unresolved resentment or anger, then the portrait will be more balanced, but some writers do not agree that this stage is necessary. However, when characters are presented as all bad or all dark, they become less believable. If your unresolved feelings about someone in your memoir are a problem for you, try some of the techniques about writing to heal in the following chapter, Step Eight, and consider getting professional help to support you as you work out unresolved issues.

The Opinion of Friends, Peers, and Writer's Groups

After you have completed several drafts and sorted through some of the narrative and characterization issues, you can have your friends, peers, or writer's group read the whole book from start to finish. Supply them with questions you have about your manuscript. Be specific and push for tough responses. Ask them to forget that they like you or feel sympathy for you or your book. Tell them to be objective and read it as if they didn't know you at all.

You want as much objectivity as you can get to prepare you for the kind of feedback that an editor, agent, or publisher might offer. Make sure they review the book as a literary work, not just as the content and details of your life. However, if they have a strong reaction to certain events in your story, they should so inform you.

- Make a list of questions you want them to keep in mind as they read.
- Give them permission to give detailed feedback about character development, flow of the story, and plot.
- Is there any place where they wanted to stop reading or got distracted? Be sure they tell you about how the pacing and flow feels to them.
- What does not make sense and where are they bored?
- Do they want to finish the book? If not, where are they stalled?
- Is there a clear plot and arc of story?
- Is the end satisfying?
- Does the title work?
- Include any other questions that you wonder about or that other readers brought to your attention.

Keep in mind that despite their best intentions, your friends, peers, and writer's group are usually not professional editors or publishers. They have their own limitations and biases. Some may just flatter and praise, others may be too critical, competitive, or resentful. So take their comments with a grain of salt, depending on your individual situation.

Finding a Professional Independent Editor

When you have finalized your own edits, it's time to hire an editor— an expert who will assist you in polishing your manuscript. The editor needs to be experienced with the rules of grammar, syntax, and writing styles; ask him to provide you with an example of the kind of editing he might do on a sample chapter. Your editor works closely with you to help you shape and smooth your manuscript, so you need to feel that he understands you and your work. It pays to get referrals from other writers, and to ask a lot of questions about how the editor works. You want to retain your own voice and to be assured that in the end, it's your book. However, it's best to listen carefully to any advice or suggestions that your editor makes. After all, he is already an experienced professional in the field and might have new ideas and suggestions you have not thought of before. You need to let go of the idea that every word you have written or every idea you have is precious and must be preserved. Professional writers are willing to listen to the opinions and advice of others, and to take in suggestions with an open mind.

Here are some things to consider when hiring a freelance editor:

- Find out what memoirs the editor has edited in the past.
- Ask for references from your friends and colleagues.
- Request a listing of fees. There's a range of editing costs—some are by the page and others are by the hour. The more complex the changes your manuscript requires and the more time the editor spends on it, the higher the fee.
- Find out what kind of editing your potential editor does and assess what you need:
  - Developmental editing: revising the structure, characterization, literary style
  - Copyediting: spelling, grammar, punctuation
  - Proofreading: a final pass on the manuscript after it's set in type

---

Getting your manuscript edited is one of your most important tasks in bringing your work to a professional status. Good editing makes your work shine, and improves your voice and style. Once you have completed the editing process, you are ready for the next step: choosing your publishing options.

Finding an Agent

Whether you intend to seek out a major commercial book publisher, small publisher, or even self-publish, I believe it's always good to have an agent.

The agent's role is to help you find the best publishing house for you, large or small. She knows editors' current needs at the different houses, and has already established contacts with them. She knows the market, the kinds of books that have recently been selected or sold, and will negotiate with the publisher all the details that are part of getting a publishing contract.

Many smart agents are also gaining experience in how to put together a well-polished independent publication that with a successful sales record can be converted and sold to a commercial publisher.

How Do I Find an Agent?

The best way to find an agent is through the networking system you've set up while writing your book. Part of the work of becoming an author is creating opportunities to meet other authors—who have their own network—and other writers, published or unpublished, some of whom will have an agent already. The whole world, including the literary world, is made up of a network of connections—you see this played out every day on the Internet, but real-life connections made face-to-face are important too.

In the Internet era that includes Facebook, MySpace, YouTube, LinkedIn, Gather, Twitter, and so on—all of which may be helpful in creating an enormous number of new network connections—it's important to remember that we all benefit from satisfying our human need to shake hands, look each other in the eye, and connect.

A good way to do this is to participate in writing conferences. Agents attend writing conferences all over the country and year round looking for new books to get excited about, and for new people to take on as clients. Each agent is unique, has his own familiar network of editors and publishers, so you need to be open to a process that might take years, not just months, as you keep writing and sorting through the list of conferences that comes out each spring in the major writing journals, and check listings online.

This process involves continuing to write with all the passion you have to get your story on the page, then honed and polished. You need to present the best writing you are able to offer while you begin to learn the business of becoming an author.

What Happens in Writing Conferences with Publishers and Agents

A writing conference is a great place for connecting and learning. The workshops will offer different kinds of instruction about key aspects of writing a book, whereas panels of editors, agents, and publishers give you an overview of what is going on in the current world of publishing. Just as there are trends in cars and the stock market, there are trends in publishing that affect how a book proposal or book idea will be received. For instance, in some years politics, biography, history, and historical fiction are "in," and other years they're not. The market is always shifting.

At most conferences, you will have a chance to "pitch" your book idea to an agent or an editor, and find out whether they're interested in reviewing your manuscript and initiating further contact. You don't have to have a completed book to pitch to them. You can meet agents and editors at the "speed dating with agents" events at conferences. These brief sessions of three to seven minutes allow you to practice talking to a professional and learn about them and what they want.

What Is a Pitch?

When you "pitch" your book, you present your work quickly and succinctly. When you pitch to an agent or editor, they need to hear a brief synopsis of your idea and assess you as an author and presenter.

The pitch covers

- The theme of your book: how I overcame a childhood of chaos and lived to tell about it.
- The arc of the story. "The story begins . . . and then . . . and ends with . . ."
- The point of the story, the reason you feel it's important for the whole world to read it, and why it's original, exciting, inspiring, and relevant to others.
- How you plan to get the word out about your book.

The agent and publishers notice your personality, how you present yourself, your energy, ability to articulate your book, knowledge of the subject, enthusiasm, whether the book is finished, and your ability to market yourself, and whether you'd be good in the broadcast media. They make a quick decision whether you're someone they'd like to work with and give a chance to become a published author.

Because they have nothing to lose, agents and publishers will ordinarily ask to see your proposal if you pitch well. But this invitation does not mean you have a commitment from anyone.

Do I Need a Book Proposal?

The short answer to this question is yes. An agent or publisher may ultimately want to see your entire manuscript, but you want to have prepared a good and honest proposal of your memoir to show them that you understand the business of writing. If you meet an agent at a conference, personal contact might precede the proposal, but the agent will need a proposal in order to approach the publishers.

A typical book proposal contains the following sections:

Overview

One page, including an enticing "hook," or one-sentence punchy description of the book, and brief author bio that conveys in a nutshell what's original and compelling about your story.

Chapter Outline

Four to six pages. What exactly appears, scene by scene in paragraph form, in each chapter.

Sample Chapter

At least one, and it's better to provide two, usually the first and last.

Author Bio

In one to two pages, make yourself sound exceptional. This is no time for modesty.

Competition

List other titles that are similar in nature, preferably titles that have sold well, which will help to show a market for your book. Describe what these books encompass and maybe even the author's expertise, or lack thereof. Tell why yours is different or better, or both. List at least six titles, and always be respectful, never dismissive.

Marketing and Publicity

This section shows how you plan to sell the book and that you are an expert about your subject. Never exaggerate. Always base what you're saying on research and reality.

- Market: who will buy the book and why
- Conferences you attend where the book can be exhibited and sold
- Speaking engagements where you can purchase the book for sale in the back of the room
- Workshops and trainings you conduct regularly where people might receive your book as part of the fees
- Web sites, blogs, and so on where you can submit posts, columns, and free content from your book
- Radio and TV experience, including specific shows you have been on, with links so the agent and publisher can see how you do
- Print, such as magazine or newspapers, journals, and so forth, including reviews, features, interviews with you
- Endorsements or pending requests for endorsements

There are many different models for book proposals, but all basically want the same thing, perhaps presented in a different order.

Memoir writers express concerns about writing a proposal. "I don't know how, and besides, it's such a different kind of writing." But if your agent asks you to provide one, you have to do it. You can learn how—everyone does. Many resources are available to help you, from the Internet to books specifically about finding and working with agents and writing a proposal.

Building Your Platform

An important factor in today's publishing world is "platform." Verna Dreisbach, owner of Dreisbach Literary Management, says, "You have to be bigger than your book."

This means that agents and publishers need to see that you have more to offer the world than the book. Let's say the focus of your memoir is about the plight of foster children—a topic you have experienced personally, and about which you're still concerned. You want your book to educate the reader and create reform in the field. The agent and publisher might like to see that you have a blog, that you've published articles, and given talks to local and national groups.

Are you a leader or have you started an organization, business, or nonprofit for a cause that's important to you? Your presence in the larger world demonstrates that you're able to present yourself and your ideas about this subject in a variety of ways. They'll notice that you're motivated and passionate about your subject, and that you, or your cause, are in fact "bigger than your book."

Here are some ways to begin doing this:

- As you're writing your book, create your Web site, and begin your blog. Write about the main ideas and subjects of your memoir.
- Create a presence in Facebook, Gather, or other social networking sites. Some are oriented more to professionals than others, and over time the sites may change, but the fact that we are all connected through the Internet from now on is not likely to change but expand.
- Join or begin an organization that relates to the ideas and main concerns of your memoir.
- Network at conferences—as many as you can afford, where topics and workshop leaders and the list of agents and publishers appeal to you. Give your card to everyone you meet—your peers in the workshops, the workshop leaders and organizers, as well as anyone with whom you might want to follow up, and do this when you go home. You never know

who might have an agent someday or a publisher who might be able to help you.

- Practice writing short pitches. Learn to give the "elevator pitch" —a brief one-minute version of what your book is about.
- Get excerpts published. Gain as much media attention for your cause or theme as possible.
- Read books on how to market yourself, your business, and anything having to do with publicity.

Book Publishing Options

As we've seen, there are many ways you can publish your memoir these days.

- Traditional publishing
- Small publishers
- Self-publishing (by becoming your own publisher)
- Print-on-demand publishers

Traditional Publishing Houses

This is the time-honored way to get your book into the world with the maximum of outreach to your audience. Publishing has changed over the years. Today's publishing world is constantly shifting and adjusting to the increase in digital publishing and the ability of Web marketing to reach readers directly.

What used to be a variety of houses has shrunk to a few, and each has several imprints and brands. But the basics haven't changed. Books are still being sought after, and editors, publishers, and agents are always seeking new authors with a bright future.

If you want to get published through a large company, you'll need an agent, a good proposal, and a substantial platform.

Small Publishers

For some of the smaller publishers you may not need an agent as an intermediary. Some small publishers are open to direct communication with you and are able to work directly with the author. However, some smaller publishing firms may prefer to negotiate terms with an agent rather than an inexperienced author. You can query the publisher to find out what they prefer. Small publishers are listed in directories or you can find them online.

If you read a memoir that is published by a small press and you feel your book is a similar kind of book, you can contact them directly with a query letter or a proposal. Most small publishers don't offer advances nor are they able to spend much on marketing or publicity, but you might enjoy the personal attention they can offer you. And they're always happy if you can hire your own publicity agent, and take the lead in both Web marketing and print and broadcast media expenses.

Self-Publishing Through Your Own Publishing Company

You may want to hire a consultant to help you with setting up your press and getting your book into the final stages for publishing.

- Establish the name of your press.
- Learn about self-publishing through various free Internet groups or writer's conferences.
- Buy ISBN numbers, get your book cover designed and the interior pages of your book laid out in preparation for printing. You will need to oversee the choices during this stage—fonts, chapter headings, spacing, margins, and table of contents.
- Finalize the endorsements and back cover copy.
- Upload your book to Lightning Source, a reliable resource for print-on-demand publishing. Printing through them gets

your book into Amazon and other online publications, and will be listed with Ingram, a major national book distributor, for ordering through bookstores and libraries. However, the independent publisher has to be vigilant to connect the internal systems between bookstores and distribution to facilitate availability of a book in the store. Companies such as Baker & Taylor and Independent Publishers Group may be contacted by authors to assist in distribution. There are smaller independent and regional distributors as well. To find them, you can look up "Book Distributors" on the Web.

Self-Publishing Through Various Vendors

Self-publishing is the fastest-growing type of book publishing today. A variety of companies like Lulu, iUniverse, Amazon Book Surge, and many others can help you set up your book to be printed on demand. The fee per book is higher than if you do it yourself, but if you want your book mostly for your family and friends, this option may be the best for you. They will still require you to make cover and interior design choices or hire out the work, and they help you through the process that you must follow to get from manuscript to final book. Most such companies also offer you other resources to help you complete the project, such as their own editors, designers, production experts for special custom printing, publicity agents, sales agents, and other services, all for a fee that can add up, but may be worthwhile if you're trying to sell a lot of books and convert the book to commercial publication and eventually propose the book to commercial publishers by proving it has a market.

Whatever route you go, it's a great feeling to finally hold your completed book in your hands and present it to family and friends as a gift.

Once you have reached this stage in your writing life, you are ready to launch your book into the world. You have discovered many things about yourself through the writing process, and uncovered many layers of your story as you created your story arc. The path to presenting a memoir to the world is its own kind of journey, one that needs to be undertaken with positive energy, humility, and focus.

Regardless of whether and how you choose to publish your manuscript, the fact that you have learned how to take your memories and create a story from them is a magnificent achievement! You reexperienced your life, reunited with old friends and family, and gained a new perspective about your place in the order of things. You may have even experienced how writing can be healing and transformative. If you decide to publish and find yourself frustrated with the process, remember to think about how much you have learned and gained from writing your memoir, and all the ways that writing your story has changed your life for the better.

Let us look now at the groundbreaking research about the ways in which writing a memoir is a healing process.

STEP 8

The Power of Writing to Heal

Forgiveness means letting go of the past.

—*Gerald Jampolsky*

For as long as I can remember, I've been interested in healing. As I grew up, I learned that I was the third daughter in my multigenerational family to be abandoned by her mother, and I was desperate to break a pattern that I'd seen cause much misery and pain.

I'd watched my own mother and grandmother fight since I was little; when I was an adult, my mother refused to let anyone know she had a daughter. The pain of these realizations haunted me, but I found relief through creativity; playing in a symphony, painting, and reading books. I devoured fiction—in those days only famous people wrote memoirs—trying to find some kind of code that would help me live my life.

And I kept a journal. Little did I know that one day there would be programs all over the country about therapeutic journaling, art therapy, and bibliotherapy.

As a "wounded healer" I became a therapist, and learned how the sacred and mysterious process of psychotherapy facilitates healing. Being a client while working as a therapist gave me a unique perspective and a deep respect for the healing process. It was clear that sharing stories in the therapy hour helped people break through walls of silence and shame into a previously unknown freedom of expression, healing wounds long suppressed and buried and wordless.

During those years, I poured out the feelings, thoughts, drawings, and the stories of my life into those journals, gathered them into boxes, and put them away for a long time. But the process of finding words and even writing stories was a way for me to see past the darkness and find some light throughout the losses and traumas I experienced from a mother and grandmother who turned out to be mentally ill.

I often felt alone in the struggle, but at least I had my journal. One of the therapies I experienced had us write the dark stories of our lives, the ones we'd been trying to escape. The leaders of the therapy process insisted that we must write all the ways we had suffered or been traumatized in exact detail. Although this was grueling and difficult, it paved the way for resolution and forgiveness later in the process. I experienced profound relief and appreciated the insights of digging deep into tough truths, and having others understand and witness me for the first time. Thus was born my certainty that writing needed to be a part of the healing process, but there was no scientific evidence to prove it—only my experience and the stories of others who were journaling.

The Research on Writing That Heals

A few years ago, studies about how writing influenced the process of healing began to be publicized in the press. The studies talked about how the power of using words, particularly writing, helps to heal emotional distress, trauma, and various physical ailments.

Recent developments in technology have made it possible to study how patterns in the brain are affected by words, and these studies are still yielding their results.

The Early Studies

As a therapist, I'd learned about Wilhelm Reich; Alexander Lowen, who carried Reich's work into bioenergetic therapy; Arthur Janov, who created primal scream therapy; and other body workers, including Peter Levine and Babette Rothschild. Their theories have to do with how trauma and stress are suppressed in the body, causing emotional and physical reactions that talk therapy doesn't touch.

These therapies include special breathing and body-oriented techniques to help the client release the pent-up emotions that have been lodged in the body and in the unconscious mind. Most of my clients had been severely abused as children, and seemed stuck in their bodily and emotional memories. I thought it was important to explore different ways to help them, so I studied these alternative approaches in the field of holistic health as I searched for integrative ways of helping people to change their lives for the better.

So it was with eagerness and surprise that I discovered the research showing that writing true stories about significant and meaningful events in their lives helped people heal not only mentally but physically. For example, in 1999, an article by Joshua Smyth in the *Journal of the American Medical Association* discussed the positive effects of expressive writing on arthritis and asthma sufferers. Discovering that writing was a factor in healing physical illnesses and trauma was big news to the medical and psychological community.

Dr. James Pennebaker's Broad Research

As I searched for more studies, I discovered the work of Dr. James Pennebaker, the chair of the psychology program at the University of Texas. In the 1990s, he began to be curious whether writing about important and painful feelings would offer the same relief as talking. He and his colleagues investigated the therapeutic benefits of writing in various settings and with a large range of populations across different social classes and demographics, including prisoners and crime victims, arthritis and chronic-pain sufferers, new mothers, and people with various physical illnesses.

During the experiments, members of the control group were instructed to write lists or plans for the day. The expressive writing group received the following directions:

> *For the next four days, I would like you to write about your very deepest thoughts and feelings about the most traumatic experience of your entire life. In your writing, I'd like you to really let go and explore your very deepest emotions and thoughts. You might tie your topic to your relationships with others, including parents, lovers, friends, or relatives; to your past, your present, or your future; or to who you have been, who you would like to be, or who you are now. You may write about the same general issues or experiences on all days of writing or on different traumas each day. All of your writing will be completely confidential.*

Both groups wrote for fifteen minutes on each of the four days of the study. The intensity and depth of the trauma expressed in the subjects' stories impressed and surprised Pennebaker. They wrote about tragic and traumatic events, such as depression, rape, suicide attempts, child sexual and physical abuse, drug use, and family violence. They often wrote of powerful emotions associated with these stories. Sometimes they left the sessions in tears, but they eagerly continued the experiment. No one suffered any adverse effects from the writing, and many reported emotional relief at finally writing out deeply buried secrets. The research results showed a significantly reduced number of doctor's visits, and improvements in health markers. In another study of the group who wrote, there was a significant increase of the T-cell count, showing improvement in the immune system.

In his book *Opening Up: The Healing Power of Expressing Emotions*, Pennebaker discusses the ways that writing about emotional events relieves stress and promotes a more complete understanding of events. He concludes that simple catharsis, the explosive release of emotions, is not enough. Feelings, thoughts, and a different point of view need to be integrated with memories of an upheaval to create a different perspective.

Writing a story and putting events and upheavals into a narrative helps to create meaning and understanding about stressful or traumatic events. Writing is similar to psychotherapy in that emotional disclosure is a part of the healing process. However, writing is a solitary activity, done alone; in the therapy office, there's another person, the therapist, whose presence may affect the content and delivery of the story. Writing may yield different and surprising material that was not shared in therapy.

Second Generation Studies on Writing and Healing

Joshua Smyth and Stephen Lepore's 2002 book, *The Writing Cure*, is an edited series of studies on such topics as depression, recovery from breast cancer, and other questions the researchers developed after the first studies.

These studies showed that though writing about trauma and negative emotions causes emotional pain and distress for a short period of time, both mood and physical health soon improve. More revealing was the research by Laurie King showing that writing about positive emotions and a positive future lead to improvements in physical and emotional health. A further surprise came when subjects wrote about someone else's trauma—the results were nearly as positive as they were for those who wrote about their own traumas, paving the way to consider fiction writing a healing path as well.

The research also showed that people's personality styles affected the benefits measured. If a person tends to withhold emotions and be more stoic, writing about negative experiences will likely have a positive effect on that person's health. If a person focuses on negative feelings much of the time and ruminates, writing about a positive experience or a happier life event may have a beneficial effect.

Trauma Research and the Brain

Trauma and its effects on the immune system, body, and mind have been studied by many scientists and psychologists over the years, and now the research is focusing on the brain and how it processes trauma.

Joseph LeDoux, author of *The Emotional Brain*, writes about the parts of the brain in a style that invites everyone to understand this important organ in the body. The brain is composed of several "brains": the older, reptilian part of the brain; the old mammal brain; and the neocortex, or higher-level brain, which distinguishes more recent evolutionary human functioning.

Scientists are now able to study how the brain fires and responds under certain stimuli, especially the amygdala and the hippocampus, which are part of the limbic system and have to do with fear responses and their regulation. When we are triggered by fear, even subliminally, immediate hormonal and nervous system responses occur that were originally designed to trigger the fight-or-flight hormonal reactions to save our lives. The amygdala participates in emotional regulation of fear and anxiety in a complex process that involves hormones and the hippocampus, as well as other parts of the brain. In conditions of ongoing trauma, the fear response seems to be "hardwired" into the brain, making it difficult to process into regular memory that would allow the event to be put into perspective.

Traumatic memory is different from regular memory. It's as if the traumatic memory is a phonograph record with a needle stuck in a groove, replaying the upsetting events as if they are happening in the present.

"The amygdala's emotional memories . . . are indelibly burned into its circuits," says LeDoux. "The best we can hope to do is to regulate their expression. And the way we do this is by getting the cortex to control the amygdala." This means that the cognitive part of the brain needs to overcome the emotional responses that overwhelm the person. This is where using words comes into the picture.

Matthew Lieberman's Brain Scan Studies

Matthew Lieberman, an associate professor at UCLA, studies how words can change the processing of strong emotion in the brain. His research acknowledges the previous work of Pennebaker:

> The insight that putting one's feelings into words can have mental and physical health benefits was captured experimentally in work on disclosure through expressive writing. . . . In the 1980s, Pennebaker began a program of research (Pennebaker & Beall, 1986; Pennebaker, 1997) in which participants were asked to write about past negative experiences on four successive days and these participants were found to have visited the doctor less often over the following half year compared to those who wrote about trivial experiences.

Lieberman's research goes on, however, to use new MRI imaging to measure how words affect the amygdala. In one study, the researchers were surprised to see that the right side of the brain was processing language, when usually it's the left side of the brain that processes words. Lieberman's studies are complex, but if you would like to know more about them, see the Bibliography at the end of the book. It could be interpreted that both sides of the brain are integrated when language is used to process strong emotion.

Studies involving the brain and writing are being done by Lieberman and other researchers to show physiological changes in the brain that occur when language is used as a tempering mechanism for strong emotion.

When you put feelings into words, you're activating this prefrontal region and seeing a reduced response in the amygdala. In the same way you hit the brake when you're driving and you see the light turn to red, when you put feelings into words, you seem to be hitting the brakes on your emotional responses. As a result, an individual may feel less angry or less sad.

Bessel van der Kolk and Posttraumatic Stress Disorder

Bessel van der Kolk, director of the Trauma Center in Brookline, Massachusetts, is internationally known for his extensive research in the field of Posttraumatic Stress Disorder (PTSD). He has written many articles and books on the subject of PTSD and how it can be healed.

In his article, "In Terror's Grip: Healing the Ravages of Trauma," van der Kolk lists some elements of PTSD: repeated reexperiencing of original trauma through physical memory triggers, an attempt to avoid the memories by withdrawing from the world, and extreme vigilance and startle reaction. The altered function of the brain due to trauma, "causes the memories to be stored as fragments rather than being organized into the higher brain's autobiographical self." He acknowledges the work done by Pierre Janet, a colleague of Freud's, who wrote extensively about trauma, and the need for witnessing and the restoration of narrative memory.

To help heal trauma, van der Kolk says, "It's important to help people with PTSD find a language for understanding and communicating their experiences."

For writers who want to use writing to heal, we can see that the research supports what many of us may have felt intuitively for a long time—that writing your true thoughts and feelings about something upsetting releases their hold on occupying your attention.

Breaking Through Traumatic Memory with Writing

One of my students, Dawn Novotny, has had several breakthroughs and healing experiences from writing about the traumas, and the beauty, in her life. She tells me, "The power of writing is that it accesses different parts of us." In her story, Dawn explores the fragmentary nature of her traumatic memories, and how she's used writing to heal: "Writing and having my life and feelings witnessed in the nuances of my memoir has finally given the whole of my life the continuity of shades, shapes, and color."

Writing for Better Health

To summarize the research:

- Knowledge is power. Most people who want to write feel uncomfortable, embarrassed, or shy about putting pen to paper, their minds spinning with inner critic messages, which can be a symptom of past traumas. But if you write the experiences directly and with the simple language of truth, then your higher brain processes are stimulated to integrate and eventually release the effects of stress and trauma.
- Though writing may be uncomfortable at first, after writing four times for fifteen minutes, intrusive memories may begin to recede, and you start to develop a new perspective. You may need to write the scene more than once or use different points of view, such as in third person instead of the first person "I."
- The studies seem to agree that a certain amount of "downloading" of negative experiences is helpful. Expressing the unexpressed through words labels the feelings and helps the

neocortex, the newer and more evolved part of the brain, integrate them into normal memory banks, removing them from the ever-repeating timeless quality of traumatic memory.

Why Your Words Matter

Pennebaker's research went beyond exploring trauma to investigating the effect of certain words on the immune system. When writers used a large number of *positive* words (happy, good, laugh) along with a moderate number of *negative* words (angry, hurt, ugly) in their writing, health improvements were more likely to increase. Cognitive or thinking words (because, reason, effect) and words of self-reflection (understand, realize, know) created the most emotional resolution. So if you want to experience the greatest healing benefit from your writing, pay attention to the emotional content of your words, and keep writing about a particular memory until you have causally linked the events with your feelings and integrated feelings and thoughts.

Causality means that one thing is linked to another; a particular stimulus leads to an outcome—*this happened because that happened first*. There is no causal linkage between the two events in the following sentences: *George went to the store with a gun. Bob died.* But in the next example, you can see a connection: *Because George went to the store with his gun, it went off and killed Bob.* There is a link between the first phrase and the second. There is meaning and causality.

Another sentence: "That day I couldn't know that because I wore the pink dress, my life would never be the same." In this example, the narrator is linking the pink dress with events to follow. This is an example of integration, which allows the separated events of a life to be linked into a narrative with a plot. In this way, we weave a sense of meaning about what happens to us. Fragments of disconnected events serve to maintain anxiety and symptoms of stress, but connecting events and finding meaning helps us to create a sense of self that is calming and comforting.

Witnessing and Being Witnessed as a Healing Process

One of the ways that we break out of the isolation and secrets that are woven into many traumatic experiences is to bring these secrets out of the darkness and into the light. If we are witnessed, if we are received with positive empathic regard, we are able to heal more quickly.

Alice Miller, a Swiss psychiatrist, has written many books on child abuse and how to heal its effects. Her work about witnessing can be directly applied to our writing practice for healing.

Alice Miller and Witnessing

In her books *The Drama of the Gifted Child*, *For Your Own Good*, and *The Truth Will Set You Free*, Alice Miller writes about the horrors of child abuse and how the wounds of such abuse continue to affect people in adulthood. She believes that for victims to heal, the secret, shameful stories of childhood must be revealed and expressed to a compassionate, enlightened witness.

An "enlightened witness" is someone trained to fully understand the painful story we need to tell and to see us with compassion and empathy. The enlightened witness sees us as the whole, beautiful being that we are, not just someone who was wounded. Miller says, "Therapists can qualify as enlightened witnesses, as do well-informed and open-minded teachers, lawyers, counselors, and writers."

So many children suffer in silence, afraid to reveal to anyone else the truths of how they live behind the closed doors of the family, when disobeying family rules of loyalty can lead to punishment. But Miller says that when we were young, if someone, either from outside the family or a family member, knows of our abuse or unhappiness, and if they respond in some way with compassion or kindness, we're less likely to become trapped in the darkness of the trauma. Some of us might have been lucky enough to encounter an aunt, uncle, grandparent, or teacher in that role, as Miller writes:

"A *helping witness* is a person who stands by an abused child . . . offering support and acting as a balance against the cruelty otherwise dominant in the child's everyday life."

When we write for ourselves, we witness ourselves in a new way, and when we share our work in a group, usually the first stage of trying out our writing on the world, we are witnessed by them. Be sure to have a trustworthy group as part of your support team. It's important to have partners in the creative endeavor with you.

Witnessing Ourselves Through Creativity and Story

Memoir writing gives you the opportunity to write the stories that have never been written before and to be witnessed by others. There are many ways that our ideas and our creativity can be witnessed— story writing, plays, music, art—any creation that expresses who we are. Artistic expression and creativity invite a whole new part of ourselves to come forward as we strike the spark of inner wisdom and vision that is our birthright. When we write memoir, we explore our identity as both narrator and protagonist of the story. In this way, we use story as witness, seeing ourselves through different points of view—then, now, and through the eyes of other characters.

In a memoir, the "I" of the story is really two parts of yourself— the character "I" is the protagonist of the story, whereas the narrator "I" sees the story through the lens of camera, observing and understanding through the perspective of the person writing the story in the present. The narrator presents the "I" of a former historical self with an understanding that the character did not have when the story took place.

This split self, the "I" of that former time is being witnessed by you now. Because you're older, wiser, and have more understanding of the plot of your life, you see yourself with new insight, compassion, and perspective.

Another way that writing heals: you enter the dream of your life again as you visualize the scenes that you write. The most powerful way to bring healing through writing is to use specific details as if you were creating a movie set. All the furniture, scents, settings, time, place, and scenes must be as accurate as possible. Some memoir writers enter a meditative state of reverie in order to bring these details to mind. If you write quickly as if taking a series of quick snapshots, you can find yourself meandering across the borders of time until you are there, again, in that time and place, in the smaller body of the child that you were, but your older self is there too. You're safe; you're being witnessed by your adult, wise self.

> *Having my writing witnessed gave me the strength to go deeper into my life story. Through being witnessed, I found my inner voice and my critical editor was silenced.*
>
> —Helen Lowery, student

How Story Reweaves Autobiographical Memory

Van der Kolk says that in order to heal the holes in our narrative, we need to create autobiographical memory. Weaving back and forth in time, we pause to create a scene that we inhabited as an earlier self. As we step back to reflect and react to what we put on the page, we're creating a new and different story from the one we've had in our head for many years. We are taking the timeless nature of free-floating memories and giving them form in the story world. We create a beginning, middle, and end. We shape the scenes in ways that have been spoken of in previous chapters, with an eye toward plot.

We make choices about what we say and how we say it. In doing so, we take the stuck memories out of the area of the brain where they have continued to wound us over and over again, and begin to make ourselves the author, literally, of our lives. We have the power finally to say our piece, to speak our truths.

The narrator is always treating the child's story with great care. The narrator may weep for that child's plight as he never could before, thus cleansing the darkness of the past and making room for new feelings and insights. Writing our story gives us new freedoms and strength. We can move from grudges to forgiveness, from anger to joy, from hate to love. When we create movement the old glaciers shift, and the earth reveals its hidden riches.

Marina Nemat Talks About Healing Traumatic Memory

I interviewed Marina Nemat, author of *Prisoner of Tehran*, about being tortured in the Evin prison in Tehran when she was a teenager. She speaks about these events, and how writing helped her to heal.

> [W]e were arrested, thousands of us, and we were put in prison. The prison I was in, in Iran, was built during the time of the Shah, and it was where people were tortured and executed. During the time that I was there, the conditions were even worse. In this prison, in one of these cells, there used to be five or six prisoners. During my time, there were sixty or seventy of us. It was this overflow of people, and the authorities didn't know what to do with them, so we had mass executions every day. People were just being killed because there was nowhere to put them. It was that bad . . . . I somehow survived this madness and came out. I was sixteen when I was arrested and I was eighteen when I was released, so I spent two years and two months in prison. I came home after this nightmare, after these two years in hell. . . .

> When I wrote Prisoner of Tehran, I entered that world, the world of the sixteen-year-old, simply because for almost twenty years I had not dealt with it. I made the decision that I needed to go back and I need to figure out what happened, because I couldn't understand what happened. As a sixteen-year-old you react, you don't analyze. You don't have the perspective to

analyze. One event comes after the other, after the other, after the other, and you just simply react to them. So, now when I look at Prisoner of Tehran, I see that this is exactly what it is. It's a chain of events told from that very place that I was in at the age of sixteen. When I look at it now, it's not a forty-two-year-old who is telling this story. It's the sixteen-year-old. . . .

What I really want people to know is that, at the beginning, if you've had this extreme trauma in your life, don't think about your audience. The audience doesn't matter. The audience doesn't matter at all. It's about you. It's all about you. You need to understand who you are. You need to understand what happened to you. You owe that to yourself before you need to explain anything to the world. Who cares? At that stage, it's a very selfish project. You need to help yourself because nobody else is helping you, so just get out there and do it.

When we say healing process, in North America we're used to taking an Advil and all this other medication, and feeling better overnight. This doesn't work that way. In order to really help yourself, you have to invest time, money, and a lot of pain that goes with it. This is a journey. This is a journey through which you will find yourself. You will find out who you are. You will find out why you are here. Then, once you have figured that out, then you can use that experience to help other people like you. But at the beginning, you're just trying to help yourself, and that's a fact. If, from the very beginning, you think about your audience, it's going to turn into a mess because you can't be honest.

The story is there, and now I have been able to rise above. It's there. I'm here, and I'm okay. Now I can use this thing over which I have control. I can use it. I can rewrite it. I can make something good out of a very bad, bad thing. Having that power to change a horrible thing, something that, it doesn't matter how you look at it, it was awful. Having that power, you kind of *become godly in a way. As a survivor, because I survived this, this is what I survived, but now I have power over it, and I can use it to make changes to the world. Not only to myself and to my family, that's where I start, but then I can expand the circle, and I can make changes to the present and to the future using that awful thing that happened. Finding that out, realizing that you are capable of doing this, is an amazing thing, but you have to go through the whole process in order to get there.*

The Narrative Arc of Healing

We have already examined how we need to pay attention to the arc of plot and story. It's helpful to think about a healing arc as we develop our stories about healing. When we need to heal a wound that has been festering, we begin in the chaos of darkness, pain, grief, and anger. As we begin to tell our story, we weave together our memories and reflections of scenes, people, events, and feelings and find ourselves in the middle of our story. Once more we are in the moments that shaped us, and even if darkness surrounds us, we begin to remember the good times, we start to feel who we are, we get in touch with the authentic voice and self that we always have been. It can be a spiritual experience to find our way through all the layers of our story and finally say the things that need to be said.

The arc of healing takes us from pain to awareness and then to a new energy of being who we really are. We integrate all aspects of our experiences and find a new way to live in our own skin. Our creativity begins to flower as we write, and we discover positive traits in ourselves and others that might have been difficult for us to see earlier.

At the later stages of the narrative arc, issues of family and social injustice may make their way to the surface, and we find ourselves confronting the complex issue of forgiveness. Perhaps we need to be forgiven, or we may realize that we need to forgive someone else for how they've wounded us. Through story we discover and sort through the threads of darkness and light, and integrate it all into a new place of strength and possibility.

At the healed end of the arc, we find comfort, positive peace, and calm, and we find love, compassion, and forgiveness, if we are lucky. However, we have a choice about how far we wish to use writing to explore how to forgive, and whether to forgive. We may need to write many of our stories repeatedly in order to find some kind of release into forgiveness or a sense of love. Some spiritual teachers and mentors recommend attempting to find this kind of release, as it frees us from the tension and the relentless darkness of the past.

At the far end of the arc of healing are the qualities that Maslow felt were ideals that the actualized person would strive for. Let's look at these qualities and contemplate how we might write about them and receive them deeper into our lives.

A Forgiveness Process

There are many techniques we can use to forgive, from writing what is called an "unsent letter" to coming from the point of view of the person with whom you're angry. The point is to express yourself fully in a safe way and then try to stand in the shoes of the other person.

Forgiveness Through Unsent Letters

If you have been injured by the behavior of another, write a letter expressing everything fully and with exact details. Be sure to create the setting: the time, place, location—the entire scene—of what happened, how it happened, and your conclusions. Write how you felt about yourself and the other person. Be thorough and specific.

Write this letter to the person who you feel injured you, but don't send it. Put it aside in your journal or another private place. You may have to write several versions to get everything said the way you need to say it. Don't cut this process short. Continue to write different versions of the letter, ferreting out any hidden resentment until you feel complete.

After that, switch roles. Imagine being in the shoes of your letter recipient. Now, write a response you imagine that person would give you if you were sitting face-to-face.

Next, write the response you want to receive from that person, whether or not you feel he or she will give it to you. Write what you want to hear; write what you need to hear. Continue writing until you feel complete with the exercise.

A Forgiveness Conversation

Sometimes we may need to write a letter that we feel is important to send, or have a conversation that ideally can lead to forgiveness and a lightening of the burdens of the past.

If you are the one asking for forgiveness from someone you injured, it helps to

- Acknowledge the other person's feelings with empathy, saying something like, "I understand it hurt your feelings when I . . ."
- Apologize and ask for forgiveness, but only if you are sincere about it. Clearly say, "I am sorry. Please forgive me." This needs to be a genuine response from your heart, and you must realize that the other person may not choose to respond positively. You are taking an emotional risk. Do not expect that the other person will grant forgiveness immediately. It may take time.
- Don't make excuses. Any explanation can slide into an excuse, which takes away from the apology.

If you are in the position of offering forgiveness

- Express what hurt you; be specific.
- When you are angry, choose words that state your anger clearly and simply.
- Ask if the other person understands what you are saying; have the other person repeat your communication back to you.
- Consider your response carefully. If you can't genuinely forgive the person, don't pretend and don't be dishonest. Although the petitioner may have waited a long time to request forgiveness, don't feel pressured to forgive unless you really mean it.
- When you do feel that you can forgive, express yourself clearly. Communicate your understanding or empathy. Forgiveness is a great gift. By giving it, you bring balance back to the relationship.

Love

When we have written the stories that are important to us, we may feel some old ice floes thawing. We might begin to feel love toward someone whom we'd forgotten, or toward someone we have forgiven or who has forgiven us.

What is love? There are so many definitions, but we can think about the possibilities: from bear hugs to looking into the eyes of our beloved, from dark chocolate to a sense of unity with God and nature. Love is becoming more selfless and connected, getting outside your own ego. Love is petting a cat or dog. Love is the transcendental experience of spring rain, snow on bare trees, exalting joyous music. Love is a healing force in the universe, shining its light into dark corners. Love is expansive and empathic; it understands and gathers in the lost and lonely. Love is connection and beauty, acceptance and courage. Love is the opposite of fear; it is like a prism, each facet reflecting a different color of light. Love is . . . many things.

Thich Nhat Hanh, a Vietnamese Buddhist teacher, writes in his book *Teachings on Love*: "Happiness is only possible with true love. True love has the power to heal and transform situations around us and bring deep meaning to our lives."

He says that we can learn to practice love by meditating on its qualities. "Love, compassion, joy, and equanimity are the . . . four aspects of true love within ourselves, and within everyone and everything."

Love is really about expansion and deep appreciation. Think about who and what you love. Make lists of everything and everyone you love. See if you can expand your range of love.

True Love and Happiness

"True love is the intention and capacity to offer joy and happiness," Hanh writes. Love contains and encompasses the other aspects: joy, equanimity, and compassion. To love unconditionally means to love with no expectations of return. This may be difficult, but we can practice it by becoming aware of expectations or the need to "give to get." For Thich Nhat Hanh, love includes trees, animals, and spirits—the whole universe.

The Dalai Lama writes about happiness in his book *The Art of Happiness*. If you want to practice the simplicity of love and happiness, and counter the darker forces in the world, practice feeling love in your heart, and note your happiness about one thing each day. Creating happiness is a point of view, an attitude that can be developed.

Compassion

Hanh defines compassion as "the intention and capacity to relieve and transform suffering and lighten sorrow." Compassion means "to suffer with," but we don't need to suffer to help relieve suffering. We show concern when we are compassionate; we open our hearts to a deep understanding of the other person, his trials, needs, stuck places. We do not, and cannot, fix his problems, but by offering acceptance and our own full presence we can provide deep comfort.

"With compassion in our heart, every thought, word and deed can bring about a miracle," says Hanh. When we have compassion, we feel a deep connection with humanity and with our own wounds. To have compassion is to be a whole human being, striving to find life in balance. When we feel lack of compassion, we have the opportunity to put ourselves in the position of the one we judge, and ask how we would like to be treated. All of us are imperfect and suffer. All of us need to receive and give compassion.

Joy

Joy is the capacity to receive the beauty of the world, green trees, ocean spray, birdsong, the purr of a cat. Joy is peace and happiness and the beauty and love reflected in those around us. It is natural to feel joy and to receive it. Joy bubbles up like a stream; joy spills over and is contagious. Joy is within us and shines through us. Joy can be the thing that helps us to move forward in our delicious tasting of what life has to offer. There are many moments of joy that give us a second blessing when we remember them during our writing. Joy appears in the world and in the silences of our own hearts.

Writing Through Trauma into Healing

There are a variety of ways to approach healing trauma through writing. Here are some of them.

1. Wait for a period of time after the trauma to write about it. Writing immediately after a trauma can solidify it and make it more difficult to put in perspective.
2. If you are writing about upsetting experiences, write for brief periods of time—fifteen to twenty minutes several times a week.

3. Write about positive experiences, using upbeat words, such as happy, funny, love, peace, and gratitude.

4. Notice the number of first-person pronouns—"I." Research has found if there is a greater number of these pronouns, the person tends toward depression and too much of a self-focus. He suggests we write from another point of view and perspective as well.

Writing the Positive Stories of the Healing Arc

As we work through the darker side of our experience, we become more able to discover the positive feelings that reside in our hearts. It is helpful to consider these one by one and spend time meditating and writing on these prompts.

1. Love: How did your family show or define love? Think about the small acts as well as the larger ones. What acts of love do you hold close to your heart? Write about the love in your life now. Create a scene where you are immersed in love.

2. Generosity: How do you show generosity—gifts, actions, words? Whose generosity has inspired you? How do you show generosity? Write a paragraph about the most generous act you have witnessed.

3. Compassion: How do you define compassion? When is compassion difficult for you? Write about a situation where you had to struggle to feel compassion. When have you felt the most compassion toward yourself? When, where, and how did this occur?

4. Courage: Heart (*coeur* in French) is the root of courage, the ability to act in the face of danger or threat. How do you define courage? Write about a time when you were courageous. Write about someone else's courage that you admire.

5. Creativity and creative expression: This includes gardening, sewing, building cars or houses, crafts, the arts, painting,

knitting, and hobbies. How are you creative in your life now? Write two scenes about the most creative moments in your life; write about how the creativity of others inspires you. How do you feel in your body at your most creative moments?

Writing the Stories That Reveal Themselves to You

As you gather these stories, you discover that the writing seems to have its own momentum and takes on a life of its own. As one author said, "Writing leads to more writing." You begin to find a rhythm as you write a story, then another one, and soon you have a collection that makes its demands on you. You find yourself reading books through new eyes, and you come to understand that to write a memoir, you must not only find a way to get the stories on the page, but you must begin to create a space for a new self to emerge. The process of writing opens new vistas within, inviting you to listen more deeply to yourself and to your inner spirit. Next, we will look at ways you can invite spirituality, meditations, and affirmations into your writing life.

PART 2

Spirituality, Therapy, and Stories

CHAPTER 1

Spirituality, Meditation, and Inner Listening

In many memoirs I've read over the years, the author shares recollections of early spiritual experiences in the wildness of nature, among trees, with pets, or looking at the stars, mountains, bubbling streams, or the silence of snow on a winter day. Children seem to be more psychologically open than adults to receiving the world with a sense of wonder, but adults can tune in to moments of reflection that connect us with that state of being when we're relaxed or in a meditative state.

In my work with writers and clients, I've seen that meditation and relaxation exercises help open the mind to remembering more details and stories that they otherwise might not have been able to recall. Meditation invites the right brain and creative flow. You can read the following meditation into a voice recorder and play it when you want to relax and deepen your connection with moments that linger at the edges of your conscious mind. Tune in to your deeper self, and the parts of you that go beyond words.

These meditations are a way to get in touch with layers of memory and to come to writing with a relaxed attitude. However, if you are concerned about encountering unpleasant memories, or don't feel comfortable in a deeply relaxed state, the exercises may not be best for you. They are suggestions for relaxation only, with no promises of specific results. Ask your therapist or doctor about the advisability of meditation.

Meditation for Self-Reflection

Writing and meditation have much in common: inner listening, silence, and openness to the unknown. Sometimes we resist writing and meditation by staying busy and not taking time to escape from the demands of a noisy, outward-directed life. The Buddhists call a mind filled with mental distractions a "monkey mind." It chatters away, distracting us from our true self, a deeper part of who we are.

Meditation is a way to contact a more profound awareness without attachment to a particular idea or thought. We allow thoughts to pass across the mind like clouds. Critical thoughts can get in the way of our creativity and the stories we want to write, and we need to let them go. Part of our healing practice is to accept our inner creative voices, to hear the deeper truth of who we are. We need to write with openness to glimmers of memory, insight, and feeling.

Beginning the Process

To encourage your inner listening process, put aside the stresses of regular life and find a special place where you can relax. Let go of your busy thoughts and make room for something new.

To enhance your inner listening, you need to learn how to focus on your breath. Breathing well and deeply is the basis for letting go of stress. When we focus on our breath and our relaxed muscles, we feel ourselves getting pleasantly heavier and warmer. When we relax the tension in our muscles, our tense mind lets go as well and invites us into the flow of creativity.

When you're ready to do this relaxation meditation, find a comfortable place to sit or lie down. Set a timer for twenty or thirty minutes. After you learn how to relax, you can obtain the same benefit in five or ten minutes.

Settle in a comfortable place and take some deep breaths. Feel yourself becoming present and aware of your body. This will enhance listening to your inner voice, the positive one, the one that nurtures you, the one that supports all your efforts to write and to speak.

Bring to mind an image of a living being that makes you happy. Some people think of a loved one—a mother, father, aunt, uncle, friend, or favorite pet. Feel the feelings you have when you are being hugged or touched lovingly by this person or being. As you think of this, imagine golden light flowing down from the top of your head into your shoulders, and let it spill down your body, breathing deeply without forcing, just gentle breaths. Allow yourself to feel the warmth that this visualization brings, filling your body with well-being.

Feel the warmth in your wrists and hands, your fingers, your arms. Let your muscles relax, the muscles of your body and mind that sometimes keep you tight. Ask them to allow you to write, to express yourself. Think of being encouraged by your pet or favorite person. Have fun with this; don't be too serious. Imagine being gently massaged or comforted. Breathe these feelings into your body. If you have a favorite, safe place, either in real life or in your imagination, bring it to mind now.

When you are relaxed, when the mind and body are in harmony and your thoughts are flowing freely like a stream, rest in the peace of this state for a few minutes, then write for five minutes or longer.

Meditation on Your Past

Now you'll be guided into remembering earlier parts of your life. Follow the exercise as far as you like. If you become uncomfortable, stop and return to the present.

See yourself at the age you are now. Picture how you look, what you're wearing, the shape of your current life. See yourself in your mind's eye: your body, your clothes in your favorite colors, your hair, face, and skin. See the people you spend time with, the things you are most proud of.

Now imagine the calendar flying back to five, then ten years ago. What did you look like then? What style of clothes were you wearing?

Where were your favorite restaurants or clubs? What did you do in your leisure time? See if you can remember who you spent time with and what you did. What were your hopes and dreams?

Go back another ten years and ask yourself these same questions. Decade by decade, revisit who you were, what you were doing, what you were feeling, wanting, and dreaming.

Notice—but don't dwell on—any issues and problems that you faced during each decade. What were you trying to heal or avoid? How did that work for you? Think about your hopes and dreams. What was the best part about your life? How did you feel about yourself during each period of your life? What was your favorite color, food, vacation? Who were your friends, pets? What books influenced your life?

See yourself all the way back into your adolescence and then into childhood. See your body, feel how it felt to be twenty, fifteen, ten, five. See yourself in your clothes, inside your room, in your house. Who were the people in your family back then? What did they look like, sound like? Notice the memories that have formed you and are a part of you.

———

Pick up your pen and write about one of the scenes you just pictured. Sketch or freewrite whatever images or memories come to you. These memory exercises can help you to bring the past into focus and to picture important scenes in your life that may have receded into your unconscious mind.

Writing Affirmations

Affirmations are positive thoughts and feelings that counter the doubts and negative voices in our heads. Affirmations are a healing and comforting way of bringing balance into our lives by training our minds to think in a positive way. Cognitive therapy recognizes the importance of creating new thought patterns, which in turn help us feel more positive and give us renewed energy.

The following affirmations are designed to counteract the negative voices of the inner critic. I encourage you to create your own affirmations that correspond to how your inner critic speaks to you. If you have already done the exercises for the inner critic, you have a list of some of those voices.

Bring yourself back to the safe place in your earlier meditation, knowing that your goal is to counteract the power of your inner critic. As you enter into this space with your intention, notice how the burden of the inner critic inhabits your body, perhaps your shoulders, neck, or stomach, or any other places in your body where you are tense.

Deepen your breathing, letting go of the negative, breathing in golden light deep into your body. Stay in this state of mind for several minutes, consciously relaxing as you rest. Allow each inner critic voice to come to your consciousness, holding it while repeating these affirmations: "I have a right to write my story. My voice matters. What I think and feel is important."

Each self-affirming comment helps balance the negative voices.

Repeat each affirmation three times while you continue to bring the golden light into your body. Keep asking your muscles to relax to let go of the critic's power. Repeat, "My muscles are warm and heavy, and I am letting go of the critic voice. I will create new affirmations each time I write."

Below is a list of affirmations that you might want to consider adding into your affirmation meditation. Make up your own to fit your critic.

- My life is unique and I want to share my wisdom.
- My stories are important to me, affirming who I am.
- I will not share my writing self with anyone who might criticize me.
- Publishing is not the goal of my first draft, so I will write just as I wish.
- I can't prove my memories so I will write what I remember and not worry about it.

- I give myself permission to write.
- If memories I don't like arise, I can write something else.
- I breathe into self-love and acceptance as I write.
- Each time I write is a stepping stone to freedom.
- When I write the truth, I balance my world.
- My family is not reading this while I write.
- I will not let my critic stop me.
- My life is important, and my thoughts and experiences matter.

———————

Take a cleansing breath, allowing your affirmations to create a sense of strength and confidence in your body. Make up new ones as they occur to you, and keep a list on your refrigerator and on your computer desk. We need all the reminders we can get.

Allow your mind to venture into other questions, images, and memories that you feel are important to your spirituality. Give yourself time to explore these thoughts and memories, and notice your emotions. If you are ready, then begin to write.

Writing from Your Inner Self

Writing in a stream-of-consciousness manner about what you notice, see, feel, hear, or sense from your spiritual reflections allows you to get in touch with long-forgotten moments in your life. Let the words flow from your pen without censoring, and remain open to receive what comes.

- What was your first spiritual experience? Where were you? How old were you?
- How did you feel about:
  God
  Heaven, hell, and the afterlife

Jesus, Buddha, Mohammed, saints, prophets, and other
spiritual figures

The leaders of your church, temple, synagogue, or mosque—
priests, rabbis, and other clergymen—or your Sunday
School teachers

The Bible, Koran, Torah, or other spiritual teachings

Reincarnation

- What spiritual thoughts and images would comfort you
  when you were a child?
- Did you have positive and negative feelings about
  spirituality?
- Did you have a sense of awe, fear, peace, or comfort as you
  considered your spiritual questions?
- How and when did you have these feelings?
- How did your spiritual feelings affect your life?
- What life decisions did you make based on your spiritual
  experiences and feelings?
- How did your spirituality change over your life? Think about
  each decade of your life and what new events, experiences,
  and knowledge affected these changes.
- What spiritual texts guided you through your life?

There are many definitions of spirituality. Write your own
definition. Write about what your spiritual experiences were
from the earliest age you remember. Think about the direction
and path your life has taken.

- There might be more spiritually oriented questions that
  arise. Many spiritual teachers talk about "dark nights of the
  soul," when everything seems hopeless and hurtful. Yet such
  moments may whisper about new beginnings or possibilities
  that are revealed in the crisis.
- When were your darker moments, and what did you learn
  from them?

- How did the paths you didn't take shape where you are now?
- What techniques or support helped you with the darker moments in your life?
- What spiritual teachers and mentors have guided you in your life?
- What is your spiritual philosophy now?

Suggestions for Completing Your Meditations and Affirmations

If the dark past is demanding your attention, write for only a few minutes, then do something positive and light for yourself as a balance. It's more emotionally draining to write in present tense. If you want to put the past further from you, use third person (he or she) and past tense.

Finish your writing sessions with a golden light meditation. The more you work with the inner critic and keep writing, the more freedom you will find. Your self-esteem will increase, and you will feel emotionally stronger.

You may want to work with just one critic voice, paired with one affirmation. Try to keep your time with these meditations simple and welcoming. Repetition and receptivity to new habits and thoughts are valuable in creating a new writing consciousness. Be open to stories and parts of yourself that you have kept silent or secret.

If you're in therapy, you might bring your goals and meditation experiences to the attention of your therapist. If you continue to feel tight and stiff places in your body, you might consider holistic approaches to healing, such as massage, acupuncture, and chiropractic work. There are many healing approaches that integrate mind and body.

It's important to create new habits and mind-sets that help you on your writing path. Each day you can choose to write a new affirmation to counteract your critic. Each day you are invited to pick up your pen or sit at your computer, and write your deepest truths. As you keep working to make this special place in your body-mind for your writing, you'll find a freedom and a lightness that will inspire you to write again. And the next day, you will begin from a new place. In this way, your writing becomes a regular part of your life, welcoming you to tell your stories. Be brave— begin your healing story today.

CHAPTER 2

For Therapists Who Use the Healing Power of Memoir

For decades, Kathleen Adams, director of the Center for Journal Therapy, has used journaling as part of the healing process, and she has written several books on the subject. In 2008, she created the Journal Conference, which welcomed hundreds of therapists and healers who had been using writing in their therapy work. Gathered together for the first time at this first-ever conference, we were all overjoyed to meet each other and to share our work in using writing as a healing modality. There are now training programs in how to incorporate writing as part of a healing process, thus making it available and widely accepted as one of the tools of therapy.

It's heartening to see that the research and the work of other therapists support what many of us have known to be true—that writing is a powerful way to know the self and to discover hidden recesses of inner knowledge, releasing us to be more of who we really are, and helping us discover who we are meant to be.

In my work teaching people how to use writing to heal, it's clear how the theories of healing trauma and the expressive writing ideas of Pennebaker prove to be true. I've seen people whose sense of self, self-esteem, and chronic depression are changed by plumbing their emotional terrain through story writing.

Writing in Scene

The most useful tools in making deep changes over several months seem to be the technique of writing in scenes, and the focusing ability of finding the major turning points. Writing in scene brings us into another time and place as we experience through our imagination the sensual details of who we were, how things looked, smelled, tasted, and felt.

Writing in scene is akin to entering a liminal state of consciousness. Their intrapsychic relationship to images and memories is brought into startling clarity. We discover what we didn't realize before—an inner wisdom that can be surprising.

Writing in Groups

When everyone is doing the same kind of inner exploration in a group and getting feedback about how others view their stories, a powerful emotional release can occur. "The witnessing has been the key" is a comment I hear frequently when the writers I coach discuss the arc of healing.

There are three important elements to using writing as a healing process:

1. Using scenes and specific detail to bring a memory to life on the page.
2. Receiving positive mirroring and unconditional acceptance via witnessing.
3. Private secret feelings and thoughts are released from hiding. This promotes psychic relief after being witnessed by their observing ego and the group.

Group witnessing has a power beyond the feedback of a single therapist. The group becomes a community gathering of empathy, a circle of stories, release, compassion—creating a feedback loop that builds and develops over time.

How to Help Non-Writers Start Their Stories

Most beginners narrate a story as if they are journaling, "telling" the story rather than showing. However, writing in journaling style is a good way to begin, as you want to support and build on what they naturally do. Ask them to be specific with details—colors, sounds, sensations. The more specific they are, the more they will enter the dream of the past and inhabit the moment they're writing about. Doing this, they enter a slightly regressed state, and are able to remember, see, and feel more than if they are in their analytic left brain. You can suggest some of the meditations in the book, and guide them through a meditation to help release their inhibitions and relax them into a writing flow. In this state, they begin to reexperience the past, to have a new relationship with it, and to process it in a new way—thanks to the observing ego of the narrator.

Role of the Therapist in a Writing Group

Decide whether you are offering a therapy group that uses writing as a tool, or a writing group that happens to be therapeutic as a result of the kind of writing being done. Each type of group will have different goals and rules. The following suggestions are for a writing group.

As the leader, there are several things you must decide about how to run a writing group. I don't believe in a "no cross-talk rule," but it's important to guide how much talking, chatting, or distracting conversation goes on, and how to keep the focus on the purpose of the group. These are a few of my suggestions.

- A balance needs to be found between controlling how much personal sharing is done beyond reading the stories. It's not advisable for as-yet unwritten stories to be "talked out" of the person, because the talking can drain the energy behind the story.

- It's a good idea to interrupt long tales and excessive conversation by saying, "That's a great story. Protect the energy behind it, and see what comes out as you write it."
- It helps to be trained in group dynamics and family therapy if you are going to offer writing groups aimed at healing.
- Guide the feedback so that the person giving feedback does not launch into a long tale of their own. Bring the focus back to the person's story that's just been read.

Useful Group Rules

At the beginning of a new group, establish the rules. These are some of the rules I set out, in a friendly conversational tone.

- Only positive, helpful feedback. No critical comments allowed.
- Don't analyze the writer's family or psyche.
- Reflect the emotional value and tone of the story and what moved you.
- Acknowledge the power of the story and how difficult, or fun, it may have been to write it.
- Respect the person's family and loyalties, no matter how critical the writer may be about them in the story.

As the leader, you may want to model for the group how to give supportive feedback. If negative feedback happens, try to shape the feedback into something positive, and remind the group of the rules.

Cautionary Tales

Here are some things to watch out for as the leader of a writing group.

- Very dark stories can scare the other members. Work to contain or assess the effect of a story on the group, and if someone is upset, speak to him or her alone afterward, or during the coffee break. At the same time you need to support the writer, reflecting on the intensity and power of the story.

- Staying with too many dark stories can retraumatize people—the writer and the other members. Suggest reading a positive story after a darker one has been shared. Reaffirm that at first someone may feel bad after writing a dark story, but that the research shows that there will be relief within a few hours or days.

- It's a good idea to assess the mental health of applicants before putting them in a group. Have some assessment questions ready, and if you don't feel the person is a fit, you don't have to admit them. You might want to include their level of stress, depression, or support system, among other questions.

- Revealing abuse can create disturbance or discomfort, so cautiously guide the feedback when a writer unpacks details of abuse in stories. Normalize the need for release, and teach how abuse can be healed. Empathy, compassion, and discussing family dynamics helps with the healing process.

Writing in Individual Therapy

The research discussed in the book shows how writing can heal in a variety of ways—from digging deep into traumas to focusing on positive future goals and fulfilling the person's potential. Writing in a journal, story writing, or writing during a session can help to clarify and bring to the surface the issues that clients are working on. As in other therapeutic interventions, issues such as compliance, resistance, and transference may occur.

It's assumed that you will have assessed the client and know the basics of his story, but because writing can bring up surprising memories, let him know that he can stop at any time and write about something else if the material is too disturbing. If you're unsure about how to begin with the client, ask the client to write about the positive first; avoid digging deep until the client has shown a willingness or ability to do that kind of work.

Good Beginnings

When we begin, it is helpful to try exercises that allow to sample some memories or experiences without delving too deeply just yet.

- Write about current positive experiences. Stay in the now. Describe the room, the trees, pets, the garden. Friends and family who are supportive.
- Begin a fairy tale—"once upon a time." Create an imaginary world about a child like the client who had a mentor or fairy godmother to fight the dragons and help him have a better experience.
- Write a fictional story based on the negative memory, and make it come out "right" by creating a better ending or changing the circumstances.

When discussing possible topics, remember to suggest writing "light" stories as a way to balance the darker stories. Rather than specific and contained assignments, you may suggest highly un-structured, free-form, impressionistic imagery with clients who have stronger ego structures.

Client as Witness

Writing personal stories allows the client to encounter and witness his former selves, and to integrate them into a current view of the ego by another aspect of the self. The writer observes himself as a child, adolescent, young adult, and relives his life choices, changes, and roads not taken. New insights develop as a result of going deeply into memory through slowing down time and writing scenes. As the consciousness of the writer goes back and forth between different perceptual windows, the ego is woven into a tapestry of greater strength, confidence, and understanding. Each draft and each story creates another level of understanding.

A new perspective develops further if the client creates a lengthy work over time. For the few who will want to write a full-length work, a finished memoir is a powerful testament to survival and the triumph of creativity over depression and woundedness.

Writing as witnessing performs an important healing function that adds to your own work as an enlightened witness. Writing extends the client's witnessing process through creativity, imagination, and story writing. The arts have always been seen as one way to transmute pain and suffering into something else—self-expression, beauty, a way to connect with others, thus allowing loss, grief, or suffering to be transformed.

Writing Assignments

Ask clients to write in a journal about a specific, agreed-on topic arising from the session or in response to one of the many writing prompts in this book. If you already know your clients well, you'll be able to sense which topics might trigger a strong reaction, and be able to guide them into that material as they're ready to explore it. I regularly have clients read their writing to me in session, which allows us to examine closely the insights and experiences that they've captured outside of the therapy hour. Knowing they are going to read their work may shift what they write, yet because they plan to share it, often they will get the writing done because they want to comply with the assignment.

Before assigning a topic that might touch on traumatic memories, you need to assess your clients for the necessary ego strength to explore and write about it. Though Pennebaker didn't find this to be a problem in his early studies, later he instituted the "flip-out rule." If something was too painful to write about, he urged them to stop and write something else.

In the context of ongoing depth therapy, there might be vulnerability to regression in your clients who have had a recent trauma, or who encounter a situation as a result of writing that seems too intense or raw to process. It's always best to assure the client that you will reach that material eventually, and encourage them again to write about something positive. If they insist they have nothing positive to write about, you can have them make a list of any positive event or blessing they appreciate in the present. Oftentimes, the blessing is that the client is not a small child and that no one is being abusive now. In this context, the present is a better place and time, and clients begin to notice the current world around them, which helps them leave the past behind.

Planning the Healing Arc

Create a writing-therapy plan with your clients, beginning with simple, positive stories about happy memories, the best times in their lives. The developmental questions can help sort out which stories the client can write about.

Clients who are not ready to examine their own life may write about other family members or conduct genealogical research to write the family's history. Safe writing subjects include landscape, weather, the history of the place where the family made its home, and a chronicle of the times in which the family lived. Such clients should enter the territory of memory gradually, exploring history and digging up clues. The missing pieces of the story and unanswered questions become subjects for investigation in the search for identity and self-history. Writing about the family helps to resolve issues with the family of origin and provides a way to do family therapy with one person, a technique commonly used by family therapists.

You and your client can design a special notebook or journal that designates at the top of each page some writing prompts that you feel would be most helpful. This way, the client knows what to expect and can be thinking about the next writing exercise. Such a planned structure encourages the client use writing as a gentle healing process.

However, writing can "accidentally" lead into unexpected and surprising terrain. An unconscious barrier is breached, and new territory opens up. As the therapist, you would either need to extend the range of therapy into this new territory or change the focus of the writing until the client is fully ready to face the material. It's as if the unconscious guides the hand of the writer into the story that needs to come forward, but when the writer is surprised by what comes out—which happens frequently—then the therapist will need to put it in perspective and guide the therapy. Imposing a structure of contained writing may lessen the possibility of accidental breakthroughs, but there's no guarantee that they won't occur.

Most clients do benefit from therapeutic writing. Adding bibliotherapy—healing through reading literature—can create an atmosphere of open exploration into ideas, fictional worlds, and character types that help clients explore denied aspects of self. Reading published poetry, fiction, biographies, autobiographies, and memoirs can help clients identify with others who've had similar problems, giving them the sense that they aren't alone.

Reminders

Research showing that writing helps to heal and change the brain provides us therapists with more support and validation for using bibliotherapy and writing therapy as part of our toolkit. We don't have to be writers ourselves to offer these techniques, and we can support clients in writing not for a result or a grade, but for the joy and satisfaction of self-expression.

In this way, the client's identity develops. He comes to view old roles and patterns as part of another self, the former self that is being shed like a chrysalis, to reveal a new, emerging self.

Writing is a powerful tool. If you as the therapist are going to use this kind of writing with your clients, it's important to have your own writing practice and to be trained. Therapists who have not dealt with their own darker stories will be uncomfortable when the clients dip into theirs. We can only lead our clients as far as we have gone. If you are a therapist, beginning your own writing process may prove to be not only useful in your work, but can be a creative new process that can benefit your own life and healing journey.

CHAPTER 3
Stories from the Workshops

The stories and essays that follow were written by students in my workshops over several years. Most of the writers were new to story form or writing personal truths to share with others. Many had kept journals for years, and became interested in exploring their memories to heal the past, and wanted support from a group. They struggled with the issues of shame, guilt, and loyalty as they wrote about their childhoods and families. The concepts of family myths, rules, and roles helped them sort through the complexities of family dynamics, and were instrumental in helping them feel compassion for those who had injured them. Over time, they were surprised and relieved to discover a feeling of forgiveness and a sense of burdens being lifted from them.

I encouraged them to write in the sacred, safe space of the group as they began to unravel the tightly wrapped bundles that had been hiding in their psyches for decades. All work was confidential within the group, which allowed them to feel safe in sharing the darker stories in particular. Once the stories were shared in the group, the group witnessing began, and you will hear what they have to say about that powerful aspect of the process of healing as you read on. The writers whose work appears here gave permission to share their stories, feeling they no longer were ashamed or needed to hide their deep personal truths.

Some stories were written in a face-to-face group, and others were written for an online workshop. I encouraged each student to learn about using scenes, sensual details, and dialogue, and coached them through the emotional valleys and peaks involved in writing their healing stories. Many of those who began cautiously and with reticence are now planning vignettes for a whole book, with the goal of inspiring others who are trying to heal.

I include these stories and essays because I think all of them have something to say that's important, and all of them are written from the heart. Another reason to include stories from new writers is to encourage people who don't think they can write to pick up the pen and begin. It's my belief that everyone can write an authentic, true story, and can learn the skills necessary to convey the significant moments in their lives.

The themes of many of the stories were discovered through the turning point and time line exercises described in Step Three, and as we worked on the stories, the students learned about the importance of the narrative arc, scene, and dialogue. Some stories are humorous, others dark and deeply emotional, and some include musings about the process of writing and how writing heals or transforms the writer in some way. I want to thank all the participants in this project. I've learned so much from you about the challenges and the transformations possible through story writing, and about compassion and the possibility of forgiveness. I am honored to be part of your creative process and a witness to your using writing as way to achieve more wholeness and freedom.

―――――――

Laura had never written stories before she joined my class, but once she was there, many fascinating tales about her travels and her young self burst forth. This story was well received in the writing group, and inspired everyone to think about their own stories of magic and synchronicity.

The Wish

Laura Singh

In 1979, I was working in India for the international clothing company, Esprit. I had gone to Delhi to start over, yet again, fleeing a mess I'd gotten myself into at my job in Korea. Things in Seoul had gotten complicated. I was working long hours to build the leather jacket import business owned by my boyfriend. He spent part of his time in Seoul with me and part of his time in L.A. Suddenly, the company went bankrupt. At the time they shut down, I was left with thousands of dollars in unpaid salary and a gigantic hotel bill. I ended up having to pay it myself just to get out of there. Oh, and the boyfriend had run off with his new secretary in the L.A. office, forgetting to mention to me that he no longer owned the company. He'd sold his shares to the other investors for a dollar, and disappeared without a word.

So my track record with men was not good. He wasn't the first guy to let me down, either. I had always been more the friend type than the girlfriend type. I didn't always have a man around. In fact, I'd already spent years alone. The fact that my parents were divorced only increased my fatalistic view of romance and marriage. I figured I wasn't lucky in love. I was thirty-one years old and absolutely certain that I would never get married.

After the disastrous ending of my time in Korea, I felt like a complete idiot for having been taken for such a ride. I made a decision. From now on I was not going waste any time beating myself up. Getting into scrapes was a part of life.

Now, I figured I had two choices: I could get depressed or I could get busy. I decided to just call this the bottom and start planning my move up. Things could hardly get any worse. And above all, I wouldn't tell *anyone* what had happened—not my parents, not my friends. If I didn't tell anybody, no one would know about it, and maybe it would seem as if it had never really happened.

I called my friend who was working at Esprit in Hong Kong, wangled an interview with Doug Tompkins, the owner, and hopped on a plane. The meeting went very well. I was offered a job on the spot after telling Doug about all my fabulously successful work experience in Korea, leaving out a few pesky details. Three months later, Doug transferred me to India.

So now, six months after what I can only describe as the nadir of my existence, I was living in India, in the Esprit company house in Delhi with five servants, a cook, two maids, two gardeners, and a chauffeur-driven car, thoroughly enjoying the colonial lifestyle.

The thing is, it is actually quite easy to go around in life getting yourself into total messes. And after those bad experiences, which you know you have somehow created, you start carrying this tragic idea of yourself around in your head, which of course seems completely logical. So you go on projecting this idea of yourself into the future. But in reality, this picture of the future is only an image. So even though I'd bounced back pretty well, I still had the idea that I would never get married floating around in my head. The secret is, we are what we think, so to change your future, you just have to change your thinking.

But sometimes you need a little extra help from the cosmos. Sometimes, you can find yourself in a special moment that breaks a pattern that you've lived with your whole life, a pattern you're convinced is your destiny, or at the very least an ingrained personality trait. At this moment, at this intersection of space and time, you suddenly notice that something is different. If you are paying attention and are truly awake, something magical can happen.

This special moment happened to me sometime in March 1979, soon after I came to India. On a day off, one of the Indian girls in the office offered to take me sightseeing. We took a boat over to a small island in the Bay of Bombay, to a famous cave called Elephanta. She said it was known for its ancient stone carvings.

The sky was overcast with a kind of golden yellow haze so typical of India. We boarded a funky old ferry boat jam-packed with Indian families and went chugging off over the choppy, grey water, the boat rocking back and forth with the weight of so many people. Besides my friend and I, the boat was filled with women in bright saris with children clutching onto their skirts, and men in dark business suits.

Teenage boys in long white tunics, called *kurta* pajamas, holding hands or hanging their arms over each other's shoulders, leaned against each other, like boys do all over Asia. Groups of beautiful twenty-something girls with chiseled features, large brown eyes framed in unbelievably long eyelashes, and jet-black braids down their backs, leaned against the side of the boat. They clustered together giggling, in their colorful traditional clothes bursting with fuchsias, pinks, emerald greens, their white teeth flashing against their warm brown skin. Everyone was pressed against everyone else and not caring. This ride cost ten cents and took half an hour.

We reached the island and piled off the boats onto the gangplank, pushed along by the flow of bodies onto a wide dirt path, moving slowly up the hill. At the opening of the caves, we walked up the small stone stairs at the entrance and stepped inside. The light spilled from outside onto the ground part of the way into the mouth of the cave, illuminating only the entrance. After being so long in the bright sun on the boat, at first it was so dark that we couldn't see anything. We had to stand still a minute for our eyes to adjust to the darkness. Gradually, carved figures materialized on the cave walls. The cave was supported by massive circular stone columns more than two feet in diameter carved right out of the rock ceiling. They followed one after another across the cavern.

"This cave was carved in the eighth century," my friend said solemnly.

The work was breathtaking. I walked through the caverns admiring the sensual curvilinear bodies. The sheer number of carvings was stunning. One after another, there were scenes of gods and goddesses, bodies intricately intertwined. They stood relaxed and practically nude under twisted leafy vines studded with lotuses. Peeking out from under the vines were graceful stone animals—rats, miniature elephants, and monkeys. I tried to imagine the sculptors in the eighth century working half in the dark, chiseling out such perfect bodies and faces, painstakingly carving these voluptuous bodies out of solid rock, rock that they made look just like flesh. These were passionate and sensual gods.

On each sculpture were places that were black and smooth from eight centuries of people stroking them with their fingers in passing, hoping to feel their power. I turned the corner at the edge of a colonnade. As I walked down the rows to the end I could see an enormous triptych set back into an alcove. It was a magnificent three-headed bust rising twenty feet tall and spanning twenty feet wide. The main head faced forward, and growing out of each side was another head facing sideways. The central figure was wearing an ornately carved helmet-like headdress taller than his face, stylistically shaped like a seashell coiling back over his head. He was covered in what might have been gold jewelry. His earlobes stretched down, weighted with earrings attached to a three-strand beaded necklace lying across his bare chest. All of this was carved out of the same block of stone. His lips were full. His eyes were wide open with a look of Buddha-like calm. The head on the right side had a soft expression, with long carved stone curls peeking out from under the headdress, and appeared to be a woman. The head on the left side was more severe looking and appeared to be a man.

The way the cave arched over his head gave the viewer a chance to have his own private moment with the figure, which was set on a stone platform. At the bottom was a stone semicircle filled with water. At the bottom of the pool I could see coins glistening. Coins from all over the world.

"That's Shiva. See the three faces. The face looking at you is the Creator, the face of Eternity. Look—on this side, you will see the Preserver and on the other side, the Destroyer." My friend stood behind me, speaking reverently in a low voice.

"Make a wish. It will be granted," she whispered in my ear. "This is a holy place." She walked away discreetly to leave me alone with Shiva.

I looked down at all the coins in the water and thought about all the people who had passed through here asking for their secret desires. If this was a special place, a holy place where wishes could be granted, what should I wish for?

I looked into Shiva's large, clear, wide-open eyes. He looked right back at me, powerful and mysterious.

I paused, my eyes still locked with his. *I must be careful to do this right, I thought. If I make a wish, and I want it to be granted, I must make it in the right way. I must be sure to wish for the right thing.*

I thought for a moment. *It can't be a selfish wish. Or a greedy wish. I'm sure it has to be a pure wish to be granted.*

I asked myself, *What do I want most in life?*

I took a coin out of my purse.

I waited and closed my eyes, cupping my hands together, closing my palms over my coin. I bowed my head and raised my hands to the figure and slowly phrased my wish in my mind.

I wish . . . I may no longer be alone. I wish . . . for a companion in life. I wish . . . for someone I can give myself to, to share with.

I opened my eyes, looked into the eyes of Shiva, uncupped my hands, and threw my coin into the water. It drifted to the bottom of the pool and glistened back at me, nestled among all the other wishes.

In the moment before I made the wish, I realized that for my wish to be granted, I could not just wish to get married, or for a perfect man. I could not present a list of conditions that would have to be met. I could not specify what this companion should look like or be like. I was only asking to *not be alone*, and if I was willing to give whatever I had to give, then maybe it wouldn't be so hard for the Creator, Preserver, Destroyer to grant my wish. And maybe since my heart was pure, when my wish was granted I would be able to recognize it, because I wouldn't be looking for the wrong things, projecting an image from my past. I would just be open and pure and ready for something good to happen.

A week later my wish was granted. I met my future husband. He is Indian.

We have been happily married for twenty-six years.

Jacqueline has been writing for a long time, particularly essays. She brings her astute observations and keen intelligence to all her writing. Here is a piece she wrote for class on the very relevant issue of keeping journals.

Keeping a Journal
Jacqueline Doyle

Lately I've been wondering what will happen to my journals when I die. At some point I got into the habit of penciling a number inside the front cover of each book. At age fifty-six, I'm on volume twenty-seven. Somehow I can't imagine destroying them myself, though I never look at them, and write only infrequently these days. The old journals are in decaying cardboard cartons, stacked haphazardly in the garage, amid boxes of curtains I know I should get rid of, a box of old picture frames, and various Christmas paraphernalia, in the corner where the lawnmower used to be. My father's death, and my mother's crammed apartment, have me thinking about the afterlife of things.

It's not that I want them to be saved. On the contrary, I'm nervous at the prospect of my son reading them. He has just turned twenty, and I'm embarrassed at the idea that he might turn a corner and meet my twenty-year-old self. It's humiliating to remember my immaturity then, in contrast to his intelligence and sensitivity. I'm pretty sure that my journal entries at nineteen and twenty are all about sex, which I was pretty smug about. I was sure the best introduction to sex was to find someone very experienced to learn from. I was enormously attracted to a black football player in my dorm; early in my sophomore year we embarked on a quasi-secret sexual relationship that soon became a quasi-secret relationship and love affair. He was as interested in my privileged middle-class suburban background as I was in his rough inner-city childhood. It wasn't just about sex. We talked a lot, and played a lot of chess, of all things. But I'm sure my journal is about sexual positions and trysts, and my insane beliefs (those were the years of the sexual revolution, after all) about sexual competence and no-strings attachments and following your bliss.

I walked with a hint of a strut in those days. I had long legs and liked to wear faded, blue jean bell bottoms that made them look even longer. Some days I favored a flowing purple Indian madras print dress. I liked to dry my long shiny hair in the sun. I felt such exhilaration, such a sense of freedom after escaping my unhappy home and the constrictions of suburban life. Ann Arbor was the place to be in the late sixties and early seventies, in the wake of the Summer of Love and Woodstock. Everywhere there were hippies and the smell of pot, boys and girls strumming guitars on the Quad and the smell of new-cut grass, kids smoking hash and dropping acid, near-naked guys wearing body paint, girls handing out flowers—everyone flashing peace signs. The rock band MC5 had a house on a tree-lined street near campus with banners hanging out the windows: "Make love, not war." I can still hear Jefferson Airplane calling on "volunteers of America" and singing full chorus: "Gotta revolution. Got to revolution." And remember mass demonstrations over Vietnam, Cambodia, the Chicago Eight, Kent State, and the torchlights and swarming crowds on the night of the draft lottery results. We really believed we were going to change the world.

And I can still see all the beautiful boys. I remember their faces, if not their names, remember dancing all night to "Light My Fire" and "In-A-Gadda-Da-Vida," and "Evil Ways," riding on the back of some boy's motorcycle with the wind in my hair, rolling in the grass and giggling over Alice B. Toklas brownies with another, listening to "All Things Must Pass" by candlelight, engaging in long earnest discussions with so many of them about our hopes and dreams and the childhoods we were leaving behind, feeling the dizzying pull of attraction and possibility. It was exciting, feeling desired, learning how to flirt, how to talk to boys. My journal, I'm sure, is filled with those boys.

I continued to date other people. In fact I dated a lot of other people, intent my freshman and sophomore years on making up for my largely dateless years in high school when I was the smart girl, confused and angry and overly intellectual and rebellious, yearning to be one of the in crowd, even as I scorned suburbia and its values. But I never slept with anyone else during my sophomore year. Really I was fairly timid, for all my grand theories, and I felt oddly safe with my dangerous first lover, not ready for one of the white, middle-class boys who thought they were in love with me, and not finding anyone else so compelling.

I married the second guy I slept with. I didn't really think about it that way, because our marriage was six years and several countries later. I considered myself adventurous and bold, and was impressed with the glamour and freedom of my life. I went off to Ireland for a junior year abroad, toured Russia and Europe on my own, and ended up in a Marxist commune in West Germany, where I fell in love with a German student who was living with another woman. That didn't bother me; I didn't possess very much moral or emotional sensitivity, or enough imagination to picture myself in another woman's shoes. After our sun-drenched, two-month idyll camping in his VW bus in Greece, he left her, and came to America to live with me; I went to Germany after I graduated college for an ill-fated motorcycle trip to Morocco where he cheated on me (in fact had been cheating on me for months: she was on the trip with us along with two other friends); we broke up; we got back together; we settled in Germany; we married; we came back to the United States; he cheated on me; we broke up; I had a nervous breakdown. This is probably at least seven or eight volumes of the journals, and I've never reread them, but again I wonder what my son would make of all this. He's seen pictures of my first husband, whom he used to call "Oatmeal" when he was little, because he couldn't pronounce his German name.

If we fast-forward a number of years to his own father, Steve, would I want my son to know that we went through two very difficult periods in our marriage, and how very painful it was? When he was two we went into marriage counseling. Once we had to take him with us, because the babysitter didn't show up. He toddled in from the room next door, happily clutching a toy, and found me crying with a strange man and his dad. He wouldn't kiss his father for two weeks after that, and at first we weren't sure why. Ben loves and respects and cares about both of us so much, is so secure in his home base with us, that I think it might be profoundly unsettling for him to learn that things weren't always what they seemed.

Also when Ben was two, I had my second nervous breakdown, was diagnosed as manic depressive, and got sober. I wonder if I wrote about my religious experience of grace during mania, when the world was flooded with light. I wonder if I wrote about what it was like on the mental ward. In both of my breakdowns, I retreated from writing almost completely, into artwork, music, and dance, so maybe I didn't describe it at all. Ben knows all about that time in my life (and in fact is very spiritual himself), but reading about it in a journal might be different.

I wonder, too, what I might have written about him. I was awestruck by how deeply I loved him, from the very beginning. I have never felt anything like the profound physical intimacy of nursing him. He was such a miracle growing up—his sturdy affection, his mischievous humor, his strong moral sense, his startling athletic abilities (who would have guessed that little boy in glasses could run like a deer?), his truly prodigious intelligence, his gentle modesty. But I know there were times that I was acutely aware that my scholarship and writing were on hold. I never turned my dissertation into a book. Raising a child was often all-consuming. (I used to picture many children, gamboling on the grass as I read books. It wasn't that way at all.) Did I meditate on that in my journal entries? Now with the perspective of twenty years, I look back and see that I didn't give up anything that was valuable, raising Ben. That all of it was worth it. That he and his father are the loves of my life. But what if I wrote something else?

Writing and audience are problematic. If a journal is meant to be private, then what happens after you write it? Would it be best written in disappearing ink, or destroyed, say, at the end of a year? I've imagined myself as an old woman, rereading years of entries, gaining great wisdom and insight in the process. Now at age fifty-seven I suppose I'm approaching that time, but I feel no urge yet to encounter my past selves on the page.

This essay itself is potentially problematic as well. What does it mean to explore the private in a public form? What if my son reads it? But he has never evinced much interest in my publications, assuming, I suppose, that they have nothing to do with him. Unless he were accidentally to bump into one in some eternal online archive, he's unlikely to encounter any of my essays, including this one, with all its secrets. It's the very tangibility of those stacks of diaries that worries me more.

I can envision the encounter with my journals in our detached garage after my death. His future wife is cleaning out the kitchen cabinets back in the house, talking on the phone to a contractor, maybe, about remodeling the dated bathrooms before they sell.

Ben is dragging boxes and debris out of the garage, thinking, "Why did they save all this stuff? Did Mom and Dad think they were going to fix this broken chair? I've never even seen this table with the tiles in it, or any of these curtains." Maybe he stops to dwell fondly on the plastic bin of Ninja Turtles, and the shoebox of dinosaurs I never gave away, before he resumes his work. "I don't think they make tents like this anymore. The last time we camped must have been when I was in the sixth grade. Will the Salvation Army even take this?" And then he runs across the boxes of diaries. He can't really just throw them away, can he? He flips through a volume idly. "I wonder if there's anything about me in here?" Or, "Wow, 1969. Mom must have been what. . . seventeen?" Or, "I never knew that . . ." He crams the boxes, and maybe the Ninja Turtles and the dinosaurs, into the back of his station wagon, along with the other things he's planning to take home with him.

Or maybe his wife's out in the garage, and Ben's in the house talking to the contractor. She looks at all those old composition books and just tosses them. It's hard to know, isn't it? They're out there gathering cobwebs, those records of my former selves, waiting to be discovered or ignored, by me or someone else. I should probably get rid of them. But I'm not ready, somehow, to jettison any of my past—those experiences that add up to the person I've become.

So I'm still wondering: does keeping a journal require keeping the journals?

———

Audrey's memoir began as a poem, fragments of memory and story, eventually woven together to form a whole, healing piece. There may be many beginnings as we search for our voice and form, and each writer has his or her own process in discovering what feels like the right structure and voice.

———

The Grandmothers

Excerpt from Nothing Left Standing but the Frame
by Audrey Martin

At the age of twenty-five, I called Evanston Hospital and asked them to release my medical records. Ten years had passed since my incarceration on their locked psychiatric ward. I began writing *Nothing Left Standing but the Frame*, drawing on poems, journals, and records of those years. My first draft of my memoir read like a long, anorexic poem. Written in poetic prose, it was thin and narrow on the page. Wanting to give voice to the turmoil of my adolescence, I completed the memoir this year. As an experienced psychotherapist, I am clear that writing my story has not only brought closure for me, but can help others struggling with anorexia and those treating them, to gain a deeper understanding of this life-threatening disease

I was a very small girl to begin with, and I experienced my size early on as a focal point of other people's attention. There was something about being petite and delicate that was of value to them, and therefore to me. The women in my family were buxom and curvaceous, except for my grandmother, Sophie, who was thin and angular and forever fretting about her size, which she believed to be gargantuan, even though she weighed ninety-three pounds. She restricted her intake of food, punctuating conversations at mealtime with "*Oy vay iz mir*," and walking miles each day after eating to burn off calories.

We lived in a two-flat on Custer Street in Evanston. My father's parents, Sophie and Max, owned our building and lived downstairs with my aunt and my cousin Deborah, ten months younger than I. Grandma Sophie's energy was boundless. Always in motion, she moved at hummingbird pace, cleaning, arranging furniture, putting everything in proper order. She was a horrible cook—with a dreaded chicken paprikash her one staple meal at family gatherings. Mostly, my grandmother subsisted on Manischewitz whole wheat matzo, dry, one cracker sheet broken in two on her plate, green salad with dietetic dressing, and black coffee, Maxwell House, by the potful.

In contrast, my maternal grandmother, Ida, ambulated with slow deliberation. An excellent cook and baker, she represented the redolence of old world and new in her kitchen, with sweet and complex smells emanating from her always-busy stove. Her body, soft, round, bones muted by tender flesh, was my refuge. At her table there was whole milk in glass jars with cream at the top, and sweet cream butter floating in pools over hot farina at breakfast. In almost every room, of which there were many, little glass or porcelain dishes filled with candies and nuts there for the taking. A stop in the dining room for a nonpareil, a handful of pistachios, red dye stains forming in a child's sweaty palms; there were no secrets for there was nothing to hide.

Most Sundays we gathered at my mother's parents' home with aunts and uncles and cousins to partake in rich Jewish feasts, taking pleasure in the cornucopia of delight my grandmother had created.

It wasn't long before I began receiving attention for the amount of food I consumed. "You eat like a little *faygela*," I'd hear my aunt chuckle from the table. "What are you having tonight, a chicken wing and a lettuce leaf?" Everyone would laugh. My reputation as a small eater was an anomaly in my mother's family, where voracious appetites were the norm and competition for food was a playful part of family meals. I would shrug my shoulders and smile as platters of roasted chicken, beef brisket, and farfel were consumed, followed by carrots glazed with brown sugar, steaming rolls of *kishke*, and iceberg lettuce salads with cherry tomatoes, cucumber slices resting on plates.

My mother's kitchen was vacuous by comparison with my Grandma Ida's, and abundant in relation to Grandma Sophie's. In our home, my father's whims ruled our palettes. Absorbed by a passion for fitness, there was an absence of sugar and an emphasis on health food, which other members of my extended family found amusing. Jokes about having to hunt for anything fun to eat would often be told when they came to visit. There was a feeling that we were different; it was seductive to live on less. I became very interested in nutrition and in fasting, which easily segued into not eating at all for extended periods of time. Going hungry meant teetering on the edge. Tempted by deprivation, hunger brought me closer to something I did not fully understand.

I was a member of a family in which the role of survival was implicit; Holocaust stories are a part of my earliest remembrances. Although only my paternal grandmother Sophie lost family during the war, both of my parents' families were of Russian ancestry and stories of the pogroms that ran through villages where they lived were related in hushed tones after dinner, sitting with the adults over dessert and coffee.

"We are the chosen ones," Aunt Berta would whisper under her breath. I knew that something horrible had befallen her as a young girl, soldiers pillaging the homes and shops on her street, committing unthinkable crimes.

"She died of melancholia." Grandma Ida shook her head back and forth while she spoke, as if to attempt to erase the memory of Devorah, the aunt I knew only from this one story, of her sitting upright in the dark, in my grandmother's bed, shredding the bed sheets while she cried.

"Blood is thicker than water," Grandma Sophie said to the table, while looking squarely at me. This I understood to mean that above all else, family loyalty was the key to our survival. And in between the lines: "You should marry a nice Jewish boy."

There were other stories that were not meant for me to hear. I'd turn my ear to the adult conversation, only to be met with: "The *kinder*, the *kinder*," meaning, not for a child's ears. I would feign disinterest, wandering just far enough away that they'd begin their stories again. And I listened.

"He ate crackers for dinner, that's all he had for months after he left Russia."

"We lived on nothing, *nothing* to our names."

"We have plenty now, *kineahora*," warding off the evil eye.

They believed it could strike again at any time. I hid my fascination with hunger from them. Yet I knew that going without was something they could understand.

Telling That Dark Tale

Kara Levine

On a pale November morning forty-three years ago I walked out of Presbyterian Medical Center in San Francisco, leaving behind my baby. The doctor who arranged the adoption told me, "You'll forget about all of this and move on with your life." He asked if I wanted to talk to a therapist, but I knew I could handle it all, fold away the feelings, and climb back onto the road of life after falling off so dismally. I was a strong girl, but unprepared to be a mother yet.

It was 1966 and I had just turned twenty-five, which caused me extra guilt. I wasn't a teenager, but a grown woman caught by an accident just when my life was heading where I wanted it to. In running away from my big Mormon family, I'd discovered a new me in 1960s San Francisco. Little did I know that the baby girl I left at the hospital would forever hang on my heart.

I began to write my memoir a few years ago, and began to write amusing stories about growing up as one of eight daughters in Wyoming, or exploring how a staid fifties girl leaped into the sexual explosion of the sixties, and when my stories were published or won prizes, I was encouraged.

The competing voices in my work made me wonder who was telling my story. There was that older, wiser me, a wise-cracking shut-down twenty-five-year-old, and a spunky little Wyoming girl. All of them had found their words. So far, I hadn't allowed the scared pregnant girl to speak her truths. The more I wrote, the more the focus of my memoir became muddied. I was frustrated that hundreds of pages hadn't moved me closer to completion.

To add to the chaos, my inner critic hammered at me, "Why write that dark story? Who'd care now anyway? Get over it!"

I knew that telling the story truthfully might make me look bad and would drag up strong feelings. I knew there was no Hollywood ending.

So why have I continued writing my memoir? One day it hit me square between the eyes: I can't let that young girl speak because her tale is so yucky, so weak, so shameful, and selfish. She makes me look bad, and that's why I've spent all these years trying to distance from her. But she's been with me anyway, much as I've tried to drive her out. She's that small voice that questions if I'll ever be a good enough anything—friend, lover, daughter, or mother. For the first time, I could empathize with that young woman's pain. She's never been allowed to mourn her loss. After all, she *chose* that loss, so what gives her the right to be sad? So, for all the young women who made difficult choices back then when there were so few alternatives, this one's for you.

I'm hoping her words will allow me to comfort her, weave her into my soul without judging her worth. I'm wishing for healing and resolution, an integration of who I was then and the person I've become. I need to chronicle what happened in 1966. More than anything, I want to forgive that young woman after I've heard her story, to celebrate her strength in a time of great confusion and her resilience to carry on when her life was shattered.

This was one of Francie's early stories, written shortly after her mother died. She told me that it came from a tiny detail, the pattern of the linoleum floor. Out of this small detail, a whole memory flooded forward that had been repressed. Once she was able to form the memory into words, she was standing in a new place in herself. When she first read it in class, she was trembling, but her voice was firm. It was the first time she'd told this secret about her childhood.

Cowboys, Indians, and the Fort
Francie L.

Through the process of writing and sharing my story, I have become more of who I really am, and feel more sure of myself. I know my mind and heart better, and I'm more comfortable with my feelings, even the uncomfortable ones. I'm able to say the truth more readily. I know I've missed a sense of belonging and connection with others as a result of the event in this story, but I realize that my work now is to "belong" to myself, by owning all of myself.

My life is a work in progress, as every life is.

———

The four silver metallic legs of the light grey formica-topped table defined the "safe" area of our fort. The table top over our heads enclosed and protected us. The black linoleum tiles with the small flecks of color on the floor were cool to the touch, smooth and slippery. My sister, brother, and I wanted to drag one of the blankets off the bed to drape over the table so we could have walls to our fort, but Mom wouldn't let us. Everything outside of the area defined by the table was Indian territory and dangerous.

As cowboys, we would venture out from the fort to explore. When the Indians attacked, we retreated to the safety of the fort, just like they did on TV.

Our game of Cowboys and Indians was interrupted by Mom calling us to drink soup made of dried bok choy (Chinese chard) that she said was good for us. It smelled bad. My older brother, five years old, refused to drink it. Laughing as if it were a joke and emboldened by his example, my sister and I refused also. Mom tried to coax us to drink it. If we drank it real fast, it wouldn't taste bad, she told us. It was good for us. She made it especially for us.

When we could not be coaxed into it, and refused again, Mom got the wooden yardstick. The one she hit us with. Unlike the wimpy yardsticks of today that snap in two under a little pressure, the yardstick of 1953 was thick, sturdy, and unbreakable. Wisely, Rick and Beth drank their soup after a couple of whacks on the legs.

The whacks hurt and my legs smarted, but I still refused to drink the foul-smelling soup. Mom held Rick and Beth up as examples of good, obedient children because they drank the soup. Stubbornly, I refused again. She whacked me a couple more times. Scared and trying to be brave at the same time, I ran under the table to the safety of our fort. She ignored the imaginary walls of the fort and dragged me out by my leg. The smooth floor gave my small hands nothing to grab onto and did nothing to slow my slide into hell.

She tied my hands and feet together using her old nylon stockings and hit me with the yardstick, all the while scolding me for defying her, for not minding her, telling me she was doing this for my own good. I couldn't run. I couldn't move. I couldn't escape. Just like people captured by the Indians on TV.

I cried till I was breathless and gulping for air. Yet the beating continued. When I thought the beating would not ever stop, she stopped. Shaking the yardstick at my face, she ordered me to stop crying. I kept crying. She threatened to hit me some more if I didn't stop crying. I hiccupped my way to a whimper. Rick and Beth stood by watching, silent and sober.

Then she untied me and made me drink the soup. There was a big lump in my throat, but I forced the soup past it. The illusion of the safety of our fort was shattered forever that day. We never played Fort again.

This story, like the memory of many difficult, painful experiences, revealed itself to me in pieces and parts over the years—like trying to look at something from a distance but there's a large tree or plant between you and the object, and it's at night during a windy rainstorm, so you catch glimpses of parts of it at any given time. You see the easiest details first. As you battle your way through the storm, to move closer to that something, and when you finally get close enough to it, then the full picture is available for your viewing.

For many years, I "forgot" about this incident. Then, sometime in my twenties or thirties during therapy, I remembered being tied up and beaten for refusing to drink the soup.

I told my sister Beth about it. She had forgotten it too, but when I reminded her of it, she remembered. For years, Beth would sometimes make a joke of it when we discussed our mother's ways and how it would be called child abuse today, ha, ha. Except I never found it to be very funny.

Now, another two decades or so later, I'm in this memoir-writing class and as I focused on the few details I remembered, I was transported back to the full horrific experience. Not only had I shut away the pain of the beating, which was bad enough, but I had shut away the helplessness, humiliation, and complete sub-jugation of me by being tied up like an animal.

In that moment of catastrophe, I believe many decisions and conclusions were made by my three-year-old mind and heart. All my life I wondered why I didn't trust my mother, or why I always held back a piece of my heart. I don't have to wonder anymore. Now I know why.

It's an amazing thing to recover the memory that influenced some very important life decisions. These decisions set me up in life, for better or for worse. Mostly for the worse, I believe.

What were some of those decisions and conclusions?

1. Playing Cowboys, Indians, and the Fort was dangerous.
2. The Fort provided a false sense of safety. It did not protect me.
3. It's dangerous to say no.
4. I don't have the right to say no.
5. I will be made an example of and punished.
6. When someone hurts me, I cannot defend myself and no one else will either.
7. Mother cannot be trusted, especially when she says it's good for me.
8. I am defenseless against someone bigger and stronger.
9. I was so bad, I might as well be dead.

I believe that's the day I split from my inner being. I learned to keep many things to myself. I became a quiet child. If I had an opinion I kept it to myself mostly. I learned how to bury my opinions and feelings so deep, I wasn't aware of having opinions and feelings. It was safer this way.

I wish I could say that since the recovery of this memory, I've reconciled myself to it and I'm okay with all of it, but I can't. I'm still stunned by the enormity of the ramifications—like watching the ripples move in outward concentric circles when a stone is dropped into a lake, and trying to define the effect of the ripples on a distant shore.

I expect changes in my life from this, but it will not be simple. I suspect it will show up in a deepening knowledge and comfort with the person I already am, but I can't say for sure because I haven't gone down this road yet.

I want to be able to say something about having healed from this experience, or that I've forgiven and moved beyond this—but that would be coming out of my deep desire to make this story less ugly and more bearable.

I cringe at the ugliness of what was done to me that day.

I didn't want to live anymore that day.

I wish I could modify or make the story less horrible, but that would invalidate the truth of it. I want to face it and say, "It was ugly. It is ugly. I hate it. I hate what happened to me. I hate that it happened to me."

For my whole life I've asked myself if I loved my mother, and I've never been able to answer the question adequately. I've never been able to say "yes" or "no" clearly and succinctly. There has always been the heavy fog of disappointment, anger, sorrow, frustration, and hurt. For many years, I wondered what was so wrong with me that I didn't love my mother in the way good children are supposed to. For years I thought there was something fundamentally wrong with me because I didn't trust or feel great love for her.

At least I don't have to feel guilty any longer for not feeling the warm fuzzies toward my mother. There was nothing wrong with me. I had a good reason and basis for that absence of trust.

I'd always thought of forgiveness as holding the other person blameless, but I always left myself out of the equation. What was I supposed to do with my feelings? Somehow I was supposed to "disappear" them, to swallow them, to "get over" them. But I could never manage to do that, so I couldn't consider that I could forgive, ever.

Now, I'm looking for a way to get through this and to the other side. I see and sense that it's the quality of my life that is at stake. I'm looking for a way to hold both the ugly, cruel memories of childhood and my profound caring for the deeply flawed human being I know as my mother.

Imagining the Past

Sarah Weinberg

There is no way to process the grief and loss passed from one generation to the next not only in the not knowing but in the imagining of what might have happened. Ma used to speak about her grandfather, a rabbi in Russia, who never emigrated to America. My Aunt Lillie says his son Sam tried to find him by contacting the Red Cross, but Uncle Sam had no luck. We don't even know his name.

Some questions have haunted me over the years. Why did my grandmother Esther Annie travel alone to America? Did my great-grandfather plan to join his daughter in America later? Was he too poor or too old to come? Did his responsibilities as a rabbi keep him there?

Because a cloud of gloom is in the air whenever Ma mentions him, I decide to conjure up his presence, waiting for an answer and the secret of our family's past to be unraveled.

———

In the voice of my maternal great-grandfather: I live in Belarussia, in a town called Bobruisk. The weather is cold here, so I often put on my black fur hat to keep the edges of my ears warm. I have boots on with leather soles to protect myself from the cold and snow. I am proud to own a pair of boots with no holes. I have a long gray beard that keeps me warm and *pehas*—long sidelocks—that come down in front of my ears, which have never been cut. I wear a black suit and a long topcoat.

My prayer book is my daily companion. I take it with me wherever I go. When a question lies heavy on my heart, I open my prayer book randomly and I lay my finger anywhere on the page for the answer.

My prayer book was given to me by my grandfather on the Sabbath of my bar mitzvah. The pages are worn and yellowed with age and daily fingering. I open it to follow the three daily services. And I just start chanting and reading the Hebrew, with my body swaying back and forth and from side to side.

I pray for my children's safety. I had four of them—two daughters and two sons. One of my sons was a published Russian poet who died of pneumonia, and so did my wife. This *Pesach* I say the *Kaddish* to honor their memory and elevate their souls. The first few words of the Kaddish prayer—*yitgadol*, will be made great; *yitkadash*, will be made holy; and *sh'meh rabah*, the name of the great one—inspired my faith in G-d.

When I say the Kaddish, I see my wife's face, the softness in her eyes, and the corner of her lips curled up in a smile. My son, he had such broad shoulders and always stood proud, with his chin up. He branched away from religious studies and acquired a general education. He had a love of literature and an interest in politics. His poetry showed his gentleness and sensitivity, describing the richness of Jewish cultural life in Bobruisk and creating an ideal society. I miss them.

There is no public place for me to lead services since the fire of 1902. Fifteen temples were destroyed, including my own. Over two thousand Jewish families lost their homes, and some of the congregants in my own temple died. It was a surprise when the Czar came to town donating rubles to rebuild Bobruisk.

Now we meet in my home or other people's homes. We must form a *minyan*, a prayer group of ten or more men, for prayers like the Kaddish to be said out loud. In the morning when I pray, I wrap myself up in my *tallit*, a prayer shawl, a safe cocoon for me to disappear into. The *tzitzit* dangle around me as I move in prayer; they are fringes on the outer corners of the prayer shawl, with open threads that are not hemmed in and closed.

In biblical and post-biblical times in Israel, the edges of the fields were left unharvested by the owners for the poor. The tzitzit at each corner reminds me of the corners of the fields left for the poor. The boundaries and borders are fuzzy, not clearly defined, which shows me that we are not separate beings, that we are all interconnected.

It is dangerous here; there are rumors of pogroms coming to our town. Pogroms have already happened in many other Russian cities, such as Kisheniev, Zhitomir, and Retshitse. One could come like a lightning bolt at any moment. The Cossacks ride into towns with their brightly colored uniforms and their magnificent horses. Their hooves make the "boom boom" sound of a fierce and powerful drum. The Cossacks come to slaughter people, especially us Jews, for our religious beliefs. I want my children to have a better life. This is no place for a Jew. I have booked passage to the New World for my three remaining children. My son Sam and my oldest daughter have made it over there, but I keep my youngest daughter, Esther Annie, with me. I used to hide my baby in the large stove oven as part of a safety drill when Cossacks were expected in our town because I heard many stories about them raping girls. Esther Annie is a teenager now, and she is too big to hide in the stove.

Last week I booked passage for Esther Annie to leave. I am an old, sick man. I don't have the money to join my children in America.

The morning of Esther's departure I put on my *tefillin*, the two small leather boxes containing Torah passages written on parchment. I wind the leather bands with the boxes, one on my forehead, the other leather box tied to my arm. I make the Hebrew letter *shin*, which stands for G-d's name, on my hand with the leather straps. I have carried out this ritual each day of my adult life, yet on the day Esther is to leave my hand trembles, and my arm flinches as I bind myself to G-d.

As I hug Esther Annie, my baby girl, and bid her farewell, tears start to run down her face and mine. My mouth tastes their saltiness on my lips. I can still hear Esther's voice as she is leaving. "Papa," she says, "please don't make me go."

She is my little girl, yet I force her to go. I wave good-bye from a distance. Tears hang in droplets on my beard. My hat falls off my head as I watch her go. I step on it accidentally and crush it to the ground. My heart tightens up in a knot. What if Esther doesn't make it to the New World, and I cannot join my children? Esther, my baby girl and my hidden delight. *Estar*, her Hebrew name, means "hidden." I hope she stays hidden and true to her namesake until she makes it safely to the New World. I hope she reveals who and what she is, and is able to shine on her own.

I have sent Esther to live with my cousins in a place far away called New York. I hope they treat her well. My son Sam and my oldest daughter went to live with relatives in Chicago. May G-d bless them and protect them. May G-d shine light upon their paths and grace them with peace.

Afterthoughts: It's indeed a courageous act to send one's children away. Now I understand the choice. There is a kind of knowing in Hebrew called *yadati*, which means "I know," in the soul and heart. By becoming my great-grandfather, *yadati*—I know in my soul and heart the pain of my ancestor. My grandmother Esther Annie Slobodin was born in 1888 in Bobriusk, Belarussia. She died when she was seventy years old in New York City on May 7, 1958, the year of my birth. How I wish I'd had the opportunity to know her!

A part of my heritage is my Russian Jewish ancestry. When I wrote this story it made the feeling of connection stronger. I did research on life in Bobruisk during the time my great-grandfather lived there. I had a feeling that he wore *pehas*, as is customary for Hassidic Jews, yet I did not want to leave this detail in the story until I knew it was historically accurate. I was delighted to learn about the Hassidic and Yiddish-speaking Jewish communities in Bobruisk. When I conjure up my great-grandfather's presence I believe that he wore *pehas*!

I know there were pogroms in Russia. I needed to research the time frames in which they occurred to be sure the information shared in my family while I was growing up was accurate. I found out that pogroms took place throughout the 1880s, 1890s, and early 1900s, but the pogrom wave actually avoided Bobruisk because of a strong resistance movement and the fact that it was a fortress town and a base for the Russian army. The wave that flooded many cities and villages in Pale of Settlement destroyed the mood in Bobruisk, where anti-Semitism was widespread and Jews were restricted from holding certain occupations. Some Jews were rich, but many who were poor left the city in droves. And there was genuine fear about the pogroms.

In order to see my relatives living out their lives and feel connected to them, I needed to learn about everyday life in Bobruisk, what type of a town it was, and its history. Through doing the research about my past and my roots to write this story, I experienced a sense of completeness that I'd never known before.

It isn't often that I've had family members write stories and share them with me, but when it happens, it gives a well-rounded view of the family dynamics. Next, two sisters present different ways to write a story based on true events. Betsy and Dianne write about their father, a figure who was problematic for both of them. Betsy chose a fictionalized approach, and Dianne, her older sister, wrote her story as a memoir. Betsy's essay about writing the truth is followed by her story "Fishing."

———

Telling the Truth by Writing Fiction
Betsy F.

My father was such a terrifying force in our family that I had to nibble away at telling the truth about him. Unlike many survivors of childhood abuse, I didn't have repressed memories. I was the kind of kid that had total recall—the family historian, of sorts. One of my sisters and I have talked at length about our growing up. She was eight years older than I, and her circumstances were different—in some ways worse than mine. My dad died when I was thirteen, sparing me more years of what my older siblings had to endure for a longer period. It was not the remembering of my father that was hard, it was the telling about him that rendered me mute. I liked people seeing me as calm, together—stable. I addressed the abuse in therapy, and became a therapist myself. "There, enough of that," thinking I'd rid myself of my history's residue like so much chalk dust. "Glad that's over with."

I seldom spoke of my dad, and even changed my last name to distance myself from his legacy. What might people think of me if they knew that my father was a raging drunk who abused his children emotionally, violently, and sexually? I didn't want to be perceived as a whiner or someone asking for pity. Why wallow? Why dwell on it?

While writing my first novel though, the "character" of Bug emerged. Of course, I recognized right away that Bug was a renamed, thinly veiled version of my father. I didn't really want to write about him, but like his real life counterpart, Bug persisted his intrusion into my story. My muse kept toying with me, bringing Bug to my fingertips as I typed.

The morning I was to read one of the Bug chapters to my critique group, I was nauseated and light-headed. I hadn't slept the night before. As I read, my heart pounded and perspiration trickled down my back. I'd written about a fishing trip—a common and dreaded event of my youth. I shaped the story leaving out the most horrifying of the actual events. Just as I did, my little girl character escaped much, but not all, of Bug's abuse by becoming invisible. Both she and I escaped into a wordless fantasy world where dolls were real and animals spoke out loud. I became so shy that teachers thought me hearing impaired. I became a silent, distant observer of my father's violence—even while I suffered it. In truth, my invisibility and my powers of observing small changes in my father's mood likely protected me from larger portions of the violence and abuse that he served to my siblings. But I chronicled all that I observed, storing it like a dispassionate detective collecting evidence for a later conviction.

In writing the story—even the fictional version of my dad—I began to actually feel the terror from which I'd insulated myself as I grew up. No matter how much I fictionalized, the truth of my experience bubbled up in my senses like a flashback or a recurring nightmare. The plot of my novel was fiction, but the essential truth of a family's trauma and the lasting reverberations of it kept finding their way into my pages. As I wrote, I could feel the tingling in my spine from kicks my father delivered to my backside. I could actually smell the pungent odor of gin and feel the heat of surprise slaps on my skin some thirty years after my father had died.

The same thing that allowed me to cope as a child emerged in my story. I was a child of fantasy and pretend. While I could not always physically escape my circumstances (though I was quite good at hiding to protect myself), I could always escape in my mind. I enjoyed the company of imaginary friends and talking wildlife. Sometimes I pretended to play with girls I admired at school but would have been too ashamed to bring home. I had long chats with imagined elderly neighbors who sat on front porch rockers teaching me lessons and sharing their kind wisdom.

I trembled as I read "Fishing" aloud to my critique group. Would they think that the story was self-indulgent? Ridiculous? Unbelievable?

When I finished reading, silence fell like a thud. The normally chatty group of writers sat, wordless for twenty beats of my pounding heart until one uttered simply, "Whoa," and pressed his palm to his chest. "I was terrified every second that Bug was in the scene," he added. The rest of the group echoed the sentiment. Oddly, for me the feeling was exactly the opposite. Bug—my fictionalized father—like so many bogeymen, became much less frightening for me when he was brought into the light. Telling the truth, even in a fictionalized form, freed me from an invisible prison I didn't even know that I was in. I'd told the truth, and no one thought I was crazy.

Since first reading this story more than ten years ago, I've been able to be more candid about the events of my childhood. I've invited my sister and a few others to read the unpublished novel from which "Fishing" is excerpted. It's brought me freedom to be able to tell the truth of my experience to those I love. I was unaware how much effort it required of me to pretend that I was untouched by my history. By writing about it, I experienced a healing that my silence never allowed. I still remember, but I'm no longer held captive by the memories.

I realize now that my whole professional life as a therapist and as a writer has somehow centered on helping others to tell their stories and to provide compassionate witness to what they have endured. I'm grateful that Bug appeared on my pages to help me tell my own story, more grateful still that others have borne witness with kindness and compassion.

Fishing
Indiana, 1969
Betsy F.

Knox County, Indiana is filled with emerald lakes and crystal-clear trout creeks, each one a jewel in the lush green landscape. Earl Pyle, called Bug by all but his long-dead mother, managed to avoid them. Instead, he drove for hours to the most miserable, rocky-banked, no-shade mud holes in the entire Indiana and Kentucky regions. The motivation for his lake selection was puzzling but for the fact that everything Bug Pyle did seemed specifically chosen to make him and everyone around him more miserable. Whichever combination of his unlucky offspring could be found nearby would be drafted when Sunday fishing called Bug to its banks.

Today it was Janey, six, and her brother Bobby. They'd settled on the bank, the sun beating down hard. Janey took a deep breath, trying to be as brave as she could doing something she hated.

"Jesus H. Christ, what in the hell could be wrong with you?" Bug barked. His face was red and puffy from too much sun and the strong gin mix he drank from the red plaid thermos. Though in his forties, on the best of his few sober days Bug might pass for fifty-six.

Janey squirmed and squinted as Bug held the wormless hook at the end of Janey's fishing line between his fingers. "You've had about a hundred goddamn worms on your hook today," Bug grunted. "Wake up, knucklehead. Them fish are eating off your hook. I did *not* come out here to feed the fish population of Knox County. Earth to knucklehead. Come in knucklehead."

Bug rapped Janey on the top of the head with a hard, bare knuckle. The sting throbbed on her scalp while she bit her lip to keep from crying. A cigarette, a near-permanent appendage in the corner of his mouth, bobbed as Bug spoke. He foraged in the two-pound Folgers coffee can and stretched a glistening worm from its cool dirt resting place. It writhed between his sausage fingers. "Now put it on there good. It's about time you caught a fish. What are you now, nearly seven years old? Your brother got his first one at three!"

Janey pressed her lips together, daring not to utter any agreement or objection that might bring her closer into her father's focus. She looked over at her twelve-year-old brother. Bobby stood perched on the next bank a little ways away. Despite the snared bluegill and crappie leashed at the water's edge, Bobby's face wore no sign of pleasure. The flopping chain of fish would serve only as trophies of manliness. Bug could show them to passing fishermen, "My boy, Bobby, nabbed these here," sucking up attention for himself. Janey knew Bobby had to go along with the whole thing. They all did, all the kids, and her mother. They all had to do whatever Bug wanted.

"See if you got brains enough to outsmart at least one fish before we go," Bug grunted without looking at her. "They got brains the size of raisins, so it could be tough for you." He gave out a small, low, "Heh, heh," close as he ever came to a laugh.

Janey held her palm out and Bug placed a writhing worm onto it, its shimmering body speckled with black bits of soil that were like Oreo cookie crumbs.

"Now this time I'm gonna watch you bait that hook. Get it on there good."

Janey sent her silent message to the worms in her pocket. She knew they'd understand. *Poor wormies. I bet you were so happy this morning under the rabbit hutches with your family.* The worm tickled her palm. She swallowed past a dry knot in her throat. Revulsion at the thought of stabbing the worm crawled over her while her heart thrummed fear over what Bug would do if she refused. Usually if she made a wish three times, blinked her eyes, and gave herself a hard pinch, her wish came true. *Go away, Pop. Go away. Go away.* So he wouldn't see, Janey bit the inside of her own cheek instead of giving a pinch, hoping the substitution would work, then blinked for good measure.

Suddenly Bobby yelped with excitement. "Hey, Pop. This looks like a big one!"

Bug waddled over as fast as he could to join in Bobby's conquest.

Janey mouthed a silent *thank you* and slipped the earthworm into the pocket of her daisy-covered sundress. Despite the sting of her sunburned skin and the complete lack of a breeze, she felt cooler, relieved not to take part in the small murder. She pretended to skewer the bait, then cast her line out to the target spot. Casting was the only good part of fishing. The satisfying *sshhh-ploink* of the sinker hitting the water meant she could relax for awhile. She pulled a cold bottle of *Mountain Dew* from the ice chest and nuzzled down into her rocky sitting spot. The lemon taste cooled her throat and she settled the bottle between her bare knees, longing to be back home under the cool of the cellar steps so she could finish reading *Little House in the Big Woods.* Oh, to be Laura Ingalls sitting on the knee of her fiddle-playing father.

"Whew-ee, you got a big one this time, son!" Bug crowed. "Fine fishin'."

Gently scratching the soil between the two rocks at her side, Jane used the distraction to reach into her pocket and removed the slimy refugee and laid him in the dirt rut she had created. The crawler undulated and disappeared to join the rest of the day's rescued companions. Janey raked the dirt over where he'd been.

"Lookey here, knucklehead. Look what that brother of yours got," Bug hollered from the next bank as he held up an impressive, flopping bass. Bobby shrugged his shoulders. After a few minutes of back patting and attaboys the glow of Bobby's catch was over. They both came over to Janey's bank.

"I'm ready for some lunch," Bug bellowed. "I'm hungry enough to go up a hog's ass for a ham sandwich, how 'bout you, son?" Bobby nodded and rolled his eyes.

"Let's see how your bait's doin'," Bug said to Janey after wolfing his liverwurst sandwich in four bites. "Pull her in." Glaring at the bare hook, Bug shook his head. "Kee-rist, you must be flinging 'em off when you cast. How many times do I gotta show you? Let me see how you're loading it up."

The pewter surface of the water shone still. The noontime sun glowed white hot.

Sensing no other escape, Janey crossed her fingers behind her back and said, "I gotta go." It was a small lie. Only a couple of Hail Mary's worth, and for a good cause. Getting no answer, she insisted, "I gotta do a peep."

"Ah fer Chrissake." Bug's pink face pleated into a snarl. "Go on, then. No bellyaching about the stink of the outhouse or no toilet paper. Think you can manage to take care of this small piece of business without me, or do I have to pee for you, too?"

"No, sir," Janey muttered, trying to imagine how someone else might *actually* pee for her.

"No, you don't need me, or no, you can't manage?"

"I can go by myself, sir," Janey whispered.

"All right then. Don't get yerself bee stung on the way. I ain't no damn nursemaid."

"Yessir," Janey already felt lighter, and the slightest grin tugged at her lips. She looked at Bobby whose eyes twinkled back at her. She scampered up the rocky bank to the gravel path on the ridge followed by the soft *clap-clap* of her flip-flop sandals as she stepped. It was a long walk to the turquoise *Por-to-let* halfway around the reservoir.

Once out of Bug's view, Janey slowed her pace and walked closer to the wooded area. Cool shade spilled over her and beckoned her. The cicadas' buzzing song swelled and receded like ocean waves as she walked by. Janey took a look over her shoulder before she turned into the woods. *Just for a minute*, she thought.

The trees and a feeling of enchantment bathed her. A striped chipmunk crossed her path, stopped, and stared at her. Janey squatted to pee, watching the creature's twitchy moves as he preened. His tiny paws stroked his face. She got up, and imitated the jerky motion, pretending to have paws instead of hands. As if startled, the chipmunk scurried up an elm tree.

Another crescendo of the cicadas' song rose. Their music was even louder in the shade of the woods. Janey thought of the thousands of cicadas, all wearing party hats calling to each other. *Come on friends, come join in*. And then the reply from the next tree over, *Coming right on over*.

Janey sang B-I-N-G-O, clapping her hands to replace the letters in each verse. She recited *The Twenty-Third Psalm*; *The Lord's Prayer*, and *The Apostle's Creed* to impress the butterflies and chipmunks with her memorization skills.

The canopy of elms, maples, and birch trees was so thick that the lowering of the sun went without Janey's notice. Lush ferns closed behind her as she strolled along, leaving no trace of her presence. Janey pretended the fronds were peacock tails as she felt their feathery softness brush her legs. The butterflies and the trill of turtledoves in distant treetops guided their twisting, turning path. She hunted skipping stones, smooth and flat, to give to Bobby.

Soon the growing dusk couldn't go unnoticed. Janey clutched the bouquet of blue jay and crimson cardinal feathers she was collecting and stopped, aware that she'd gone too far. The first tears spilled, burning salty rivulets on her sunburned cheeks. She feared far less the darkness and the woods than Bug's fury. He'd be so mad that she'd wandered off, and with Ma and Amelia back at home, there'd be no one to get between Janey and Bug's ham-sized fist. More scared of Bug than the deepening darkness, Janey ran into the forest. Being lost, as bad as it was, was better than being found.

After wandering aimlessly and finding nothing familiar, Janey ducked into a huge fallen tree, hollowed out by years of decay. She made herself small, folding her legs against her chest and wrapping her arms around them. She sat very still, barely blinking. Perhaps her stillness would transport her back to the rocky bank where her Mountain Dew bottle sat and her worm sanctuary lay undisturbed between the rocks. *Yea, though I walk through the valley of the shadow of death, I will fear no evil.*

Janey forced herself to hold her eyes open, trying to ward off the black flannel night. She stretched her eyes wide and round, imagining she had owls' eyes. The cicadas' song was silenced and the night was filled with mysterious hoots and the rustling of leaves. The sound of her own breathing became all that Janey would let herself hear. She sat motionless, still clasping the feathers in her fist. The blackness around her was a watch with no hands.

She rested her head on her knees. After a while Janey noticed shafts of moonlight dappling the ground with pale blue light. The cicadas' sleeping silence was filled with a chirping of crickets and deep sound of bullfrogs. The woodsy symphony quieted Janey. She followed the songs for a time, unaware of time passing when from a distance she heard her name, "Janey, Janey," first one voice then another chimed. "Janey-pie, we're looking for you. Janey, where are you?"

Panic grabbed her for the first time since she had found the hollow log hours before. She held her breath as the voices grew nearer. She was of the forest now, an animal trapped in its nest.

"Janey! Where ARE you?" It was Bobby.

Then another voice closer to her, "Janey, honey, come out. We want to bring you home." Amelia, her older sister, sounded worried.

Amelia! she thought. Fear flashed through her like summer heat lightning. Amelia was supposed to be home. How did she get here? She dropped her feathers, covered her ears, closed her eyes, and did her best not to breathe. Her heart thumped and she feared it would betray her whereabouts. She kept her eyes closed tight.

"Janey? JANEY!" Amelia was shaking her, but Janey was afraid to open her eyes. Amelia squatted in front of her and whispered, "What're you doing hiding from us? We've been looking for a long, long time." Amelia, though fifteen, appeared more woman than girl.

Janey just stared at the moonlit face of Amelia, her soft eyes. How she wanted her sister to crawl inside the log with her. Together with Bobby they could hide forever. But then Bug would still find them, and her mother was always so heartbroken to see the bruises.

"Are you hurt? Did you hit your head? Can you talk?" Amelia shined her flashlight onto Janey's face, the light stabbing at her eyes. Janey squinted and nodded her head. Amelia stroked Janey's hair with her fingertips. "I know you just want to hide, Janey-pie, but half the congregation of St. Catherine's and the county sheriff are out here. They're going to get bloodhounds next." Amelia stood up and put out her hand. "Come on, Punkin. We'll be okay."

Janey liked the sound of *we* when Amelia said it. Her legs were numb and felt like tingling rubber beneath her, feeling both dead and alive at once. She took her sister's hand. Amelia squeezed and Janey squeezed back.

"I found her! She's okay!" Amelia shouted. "Over here! I FOUND HER!"

Leaves rustled,.and twigs snapped. Beams of light pierced the woods as flashlights blasted light onto Janey and Amelia.

Choruses of "Thank God," and "What a relief," could be heard from the faceless throng behind flashlight beams. Hugs and pats from people she did not recognize were lavished on her.

Bug's booming voice pierced the crowd. "Good God, girl! Where in hell have you been all this time? What is *wrong* with you for God's sake?" His flashlight beam bounced on the ground as he rushed toward her, hand balled into a tight fist, his face a snarl. "Have you been sitting here all this goddamn time?" Janey stopped still, afraid to move. Her father seemed to realize there was an audience. In a softer tone, "I'd like to thank youse for coming out tonight, 'preciate your helping me find my little girl. C'mon, honey. Let's go on home."

"Go ahead, get in the car." His hollow voice made Janey tremble at what might be ahead for her that night. Amelia and Bobby climbed into the back seat and made room for Janey.

"Go on, now."

Janey turned and felt the swift thud of Bug's shoe bottom against her backside. She peed a little bit and bit her tongue. One more thump threw her through the door and into her brother's lap. Bobby looked straight ahead, knowing better than to comfort her. Amelia gripped the torn vinyl armrest with one hand and held Janey's hand with the other. Janey felt her ears grow hot with humiliation but as she scrunched between them, she had a sense of relief as she clutched Amelia's hand. Sometimes getting kicked was not as bad as waiting to get kicked. Maybe that was as bad as it would get, this time.

Bug drove wildly, tossing cigarette butts out the window and taking long pulls from a bottle. Moonlit corn and soybean fields blurred by. Bug's ranting unbroken string of profanity filled the car for the seventy-five miles home. "Goddamn pains in the ass, every one of 'em. Who the hell needs this shit? Boils on my ass—that's what they are. Boils on my ass."

When they finally arrived at the small farmhouse, the children tumbled out of the car and scurried up the steps to the back stoop. Seeing her mother's ashen face at the screen door stung Janey's heart. Mama—she must have been worried all this time.

"Oh, *Madonna*," Ma said, clutching Janey to her, her fingers combing moist hair from her forehead. Dotty's face looked gray; her tawny eyes were strained.

The smell of cinnamon enveloped Janey, reminding her how hungry she was. Dotty said, "Why don't youse go clean up and get your pj's on. I got some thimble donuts for you to make, but I want to get everything, you know, settled down a bit, eh?"

Amelia sprayed Solarcaine on Janey's shoulders, giving her a split-second of relief from the screaming sunburn. The fresh cotton nightie felt cool against her skin. Bobby slipped his pajamas on over his undershorts. Amelia magically changed into her flannel nightgown without once revealing her newly womanly body.

When the three emerged from the bathroom, the best thing possible had happened: the door to their parents' room was closed and only bear-like snoring could be heard. Janey felt her jaw relax. She quickly turned three circles and blinked her *thank you*. Dotty beckoned them to the kitchen, holding her finger against her lips. They tiptoed past the door, daring not to look at it.

They settled into preparing thimble donuts as if such late-night cooking projects happened every day. "I just about made these myself, youse took so long to get home," Dotty said. "Janey, why don't you pop open that can?" Popping the can was her favorite task in donut making.

Janey unwrapped the blue spiral paper from the *Pillsbury* biscuit can and waited for the *pfff as* it opened. Bobby and Janey grinned as they pressed thimbles into the center of each biscuit and twisted. They tapped the thimbles so the doughy balls fell out, and Amelia scooped them into the hot, oily skillet where the sizzle filled the room with a sweet, yeasty smell. Janey's mouth watered as she dragged crisp, warm donuts through a swirl of cinnamon and sugar.

The night's breeze was blowing through the screen door as they munched on their treat. The scent of the night made Janey think of her secret log, her hideout, the chipmunks and the birds, wondering where they were now, holding the peace of the forest to her heart. She watched her mother stare out the front door, her face slack of its forced smile. Janey tried not to notice the tears in her eyes, and grabbed another doughnut.

The sore place on her bottom where she was kicked was not throbbing any longer. Her mother went to the stove to fry more doughnuts, as they all giggled together at the sugar mustaches they wore, all of them secretly grateful the giant was asleep.

This was not the story I meant to write when I joined Linda's memoir writing class, but it was the one I needed to tell. Going back to that turning point in my life was painful, but the process of writing about it was also liberating. Something that I held inside of myself all my life has been released. Sharing the experience with the group members and now with readers helped to transform the experience from one of pain, guilt, and shame to one of love and triumph.

Enough
Dianne G.

This is my darkest hour. My twelve-year-old heart is aching as I sit shivering, arms wrapped around my legs, rocking back and forth on the back stoop. I always thought that the phrase was a made-up thing, "my heart is aching," but this *really* hurts. It feels as though my heart could break into a thousand pieces. It feels as though I could die. Maybe I *will* die. Maybe he'll kill me.

I'm thinking of a scene from one of Dad's war movies that we watched a thousand times. William Holden is an officer who has just been captured and taken to a prisoner of war camp. An English officer, also a prisoner, asks him how all of the men in his platoon had died. Holden responded, "Malaria, dysentery, beri-beri, gangrene. Others causes of death—famine, overwork, bullet wounds, snake bites . . . And then there were some who just got tired of living."

That's me. I'm a sad twelve-year-old, sick and tired of living. I'm a prisoner of war in my own home. It's not just the cold war that has been waged for years between my mother and father. I'm a prisoner, just as surely as if I were surrounded by barbed-wire fences and guarded by enemy soldiers with guns. There are no German Shepherds prowling the perimeters, because they are unnecessary. We are all prisoners inside these walls, captives bound together by my father's haunted past and my mother's denial and sense of duty. And we children are prisoners by birth. The ghosts, the secrets, and the silence are stronger than any shackles.

I feel sick to my stomach as I sit. I've been told I have a nervous stomach. The doctor gives me coke syrup, which is pretty cool. It's nice and sweet. Still, whenever I take it I think, "How's this going to cure what ails me? It's my life that is making me sick." I get headaches, too. My mom gets my eyes checked and I get reading glasses that I rarely wear. She takes down my ponytail because maybe it's too heavy on the back of my head. She doesn't know that I see too much and the pressure of my misery is what makes my head hurt.

Mom had her own problems growing up. When she was twelve, she was sent away to live with her aunt, then a single adult who lived with her recently widowed father. Mom was sent to live with her because it was "improper" for an unwed daughter to live alone with her father. I always wondered what they thought my mom would be able to do to save that old maid and her crabby old father from sin. Mom hated being exiled to live with these old-minded people. She felt rejected by her family, thrown away. Once, she hopped a train back home because her aunt was making her wear ridiculous clothes to a school dance. My grandmother met her at the door, the story goes, surprised by her sudden appearance. As my mother told it, her own mother told her that she had been away so long that sometimes she forgot that my mother was her child. She was sent back to my great aunt's home that smelled of stale garlic and cleanser, old man's breath and death. She was sent back until she finally refused to stay. She returned home, dejected, dutiful child, trying to regain her rightful place in the family.

I've thought about telling her about Dad, but I always reject the idea. She never picked up my hints about him, even though I did everything but outright tell her. I decided she didn't want to know, couldn't handle it. How could she *not* know, not sense that something was wrong?

My mother sacrificed and stayed in this joyless marriage for years, "for the sake of the kids." She always said that Dad had a lot of problems, but he was a good provider and really loved us kids. This is what kept her going. Maybe, in darker moments, I thought she wouldn't believe me if I told her the truth. She did have that Italian ability to see only what she wanted to see and deny the rest. Maybe she wouldn't be able to protect me even if she did know. Maybe she already knew, and could do nothing to save me, but that possibility would be unbearable. Better to hold on to the image of a loving mother who didn't know than to confront her, only to find that she was weak and incapable of helping me. I needed to hold on to hope.

I've tried everything I know how to do to survive. I have learned to read the moods. I know how to avoid punishment and get on Dad's good side. I don't make waves. I retreat. I obey orders.

I become invisible, camouflaged into the background of this bleak house. I have become a good little soldier.

I am at the mercy of this prison's tyrant, my father. Is there no way out? Is there no escape? What is the good of living if I just survive my time here and emerge a shattered soul? This pain and misery are too much to bear. I'm a captive within these prison walls. My only salvation is within myself. There's no one to rescue me. This is my own journey. Why me? Why am I being tested like this? I carry my prison with me wherever I go.

Our Father Who Art in Heaven
Hallowed be thy name
> *Give us this day our daily bread*
> *And forgive us our trespasses,*
> *As we forgive those who have trespassed against us.*
> *And lead us not unto temptation*
> *But deliver us from Evil,*
> *Amen*

Please, please, please, let me get through this. I can no longer live this way. Something must change.

———

This has been a long journey. I'll spare the gory details. It's enough to say that for years I have caught the eye of my father. Repeatedly he seeks me out when we are home alone together. Usually it's when he's lying on the couch. He calls me over to "check me." I assume the position, which is to stand in front of him, face forward, as he lies on his side on the couch. I stand at attention as he inspects his subordinate. I do what I am told. I stand there, lifeless, as he reaches over, his hand seeming to have a life of its own. Occasionally I sneak a look at his expressionless face and wonder, "What's going on in there?" Usually his eyes are closed. He gives no sign that he's doing anything out of the ordinary. It's only his fingers that move. Eventually, by some unknown perverted criteria, he pronounces me fit and dismisses me. I am allowed to readjust my bra and panties and leave the room. He stays on the couch. Sometimes he falls asleep. It is always the same. *Always* the same. This is my hell.

I have left my body many times during this ordeal. I have hovered above this lurid scene as the child that is my body stands there in humiliation and revulsion. I have dampened the feelings of disgust and shame. I have seen it all as though it were happening to a stranger. "Stand still, stand still, stand still," she thinks. "It will be over soon." "Look at the painting of the wooded stream hanging on the wall behind the couch. Green, blue, brown in the trees, reflections on the water, imagine the breeze," she whimpers. "Go deep inside, shut off your brain. Go into the dark emptiness, like falling into a deep well. Feel the oblivion," she desperately whispers. "I hate you, you sick son of a bitch!" she silently screams, body frozen in time and space. I have witnessed this scene more times than I can remember. How much more can this little girl take?

———

So I sit outside, hoping that somehow I can put this off, or that it will all go away. I know it won't. Just let him be asleep when I go in so I can have another day to think this out, plan my escape. I close my eyes.

My deepest fears overwhelm me. Maybe I brought this all on myself. It's my fault! Wasn't I curious when I saw him with my older sister? Wasn't I a bit jealous? Did I flaunt myself in front of him? Did I make myself available? Did I ask for this? Did I want this?

Was I like him? Hadn't I, at times, lorded power over my little sister and brother when I was taking care of them? Didn't I like the way that felt, to have them do what I told them to? I love them with all of my heart, but I can still be mean to them. Is this the meaning of abuse of power? I will *never* have kids! This sickness must stop with this generation.

Hadn't I stood by and watched as my father kicked my brother up the stairs for being home late from his paper route? So what if I was six the time? I knew it was wrong and I did nothing. What if I'm just like Dad? What if I'm destined to perpetuate this damage onto anyone who might love me?

I know that Dad didn't start out to be this way. And I even know that he loves me, but that love isn't enough for him to rise above his own demons. That love doesn't stop him from hurting me. Perhaps the sick part of me, the damaged soul, will get the best of me. I'll be going along in my life thinking I'm doing all right, only to find out that I haven't escaped, but only created a new type of prison with different captives.

What if I am just like him and hurt little children, causing them to feel the agony that I feel at this moment? Or will I be like my mom, unable or unwilling to see what is going on in her own house because of her own past, her own blind spots? Is life just hopeless? Am I hopeless? Am I damaged goods? Should I just give up? I may simply be the walking wounded, too damaged to heal. I feel so old. I have seen too much. I know too much. This seems worse than physical death, so what am I worried about?

What will happen if I go in there and confront him? Will he laugh and overpower me? Will he knock me across the room or pick me up by the front of my shirt and shake me in the air while he screams in my face? Will he slap me and tell me to shut my smart mouth? Will he tell my mother? Will he say that I am a liar and cast me out of the house? Where will I go?

Mea culpa, mea culpa, mea maxima culpa.

"Through my fault, through my fault, through my most grievous fault. I am heartily sorry for having offended thee," I repeat, over and over again.

I close my eyes, I breathe, and some of the panic rolls off me. I go deeper and deeper inside of myself to where it is very, very still. I am filled with colors, multifaceted jewels around my heart. I bathe myself in this warmth. I let the light radiate throughout my body. And though it seems impossible, I become even stiller. The colors turn into iridescent blue light. I feel this light coursing through my body. I feel it focus in my head behind my eyes, become a brilliant beam of light.

Hail Mary, full of grace
The Lord is with thee.
Blessed art though among women,
And blessed is the fruit of thy womb Jesus.
Holy Mary, Mother of God,
Pray for us sinners now,
And at the hour of our death.
Amen.

I chant this three times and then I hear a small, quiet, sure little voice reply, "Now."

With all my might I force myself to stand. My legs are numb. They shake with the effort. I turn the screen doorknob, pull open the screen, and then very quietly open the door. I walk through the kitchen, still holding on to the hope that I have escaped my death for yet another night. And then it happens. I have not escaped.

"Is that you?" my dad calls from the hall. He must have been in the bathroom. "Shit, shit, shit," I panic. He's not asleep!

"Yes, sir," I reply.

"Come here," he orders.

I follow him into the front room as he sits down on the couch.

He motions me forward with a wag of his finger and I obey. As I approach him our eyes meet. I stand in front of him, but this time is different. I don't leave my body. I don't stare off into space. I don't distract myself. I look at him, straight in the eyes before he even has a chance to lie down and assume his own position.

"This is it!" I think, as I stare directly into his steel-blue eyes. Energy is coursing through my body. I take a deep breath and the world seems to stop. I wait until I am ready and then time starts again in slow motion. My senses are all heightened. And then my voice emerges.

"ENOUGH!" I command. He stares back at me, his eyes menacing, a slight sneer on his mouth. But I also see something else there. Fear. Neither of us moves.

"You will NEVER touch me again!"

I continue to stare at him for what seems like an eternity. I want to make sure he has gotten my message. I can hear him breathing. The air between us is thick. I hear the clock ticking on the wall, the distant street noises, and still I stare. And then he glances away. No more words are spoken. I turn and walk away, not waiting to be dismissed.

As Helen was exploring her family history in the memoir class, she realized her experiences with spirituality were important, so she began a series of stories about her Native American roots and traditions. This is the first story of the series.

The Center of the Universe
Helen Lowery

Most of my life I've been searching for where I belong. I've always had a deeply felt connection with the earth, wind, water, animals, mountains—but not so much with my family of origin. Having been born in the country, I'd stay outside from the time I woke up until the time I went to bed. My favorite place as a child was a cave I dug in the side of the hill down from our house. I covered the cave with tree limbs, dirt, and dead leaves, so no one would know I was there. This little cave was where I dreamed of different days to come when I'd feel at home and safe.

Time passed, and I married and had children, but whenever I needed solace, in my mind I'd return to my cave. Since I was nine or ten, I'd been looking for my Native American roots, but without a reservation number it was hard to prove whether or not I was Native American. My Dad refused to talk about his family, though I'd learned all of my native ways from him while hunting and fishing as a child. Unconsciously, I must have been looking for the loose-hanging connections of my feelings about my native blood, feeling like I was a car without any gas, that I was not doing what I'd been created to do.

Vickie, one of the nurses where I worked, was a registered Iroquois and her mother was a full-blooded Iroquois. On July 4, 1984, Vickie invited me to go to a powwow in the far northeastern corner of Oklahoma. The powwow was on the Cherokee Tahlequah Reservation where my paternal grandmother told me my great-grandparents had been relocated in 1830 during the Trail of Tears. The Trail of Tears was a government-forced migration of

Native American tribes who walked from their homeland in the Southeast of the United State to Tahlequah, Oklahoma, at the point of a gun. Many of the old people and children died along the way due to exposure, tainted food, limited supplies, and disease, but our family made it to Tahlequah.

On this hot and hazy holiday weekend, Vicki and I left North Dallas, and sat in bumper-to-bumper traffic with the windows down drinking ice cold beer and listening to drumming music. When we finally broke out of the clutches of North Dallas, we drove north on Interstate 35 and finally left the freeway. Vicki's little Honda hummed around hilly, sharp two-lane highways with no shoulder through heavily wooded landscapes. The wind in my face was fresh and more breathable than the smoggy Dallas air. As we rose over a hill, the landscape opened up with fields of gold. Abruptly the little car shuddered to a halt off the side of the road next to a barbed-wire fence. The cattle looked up from their grazing to see what was going on.

"Why are we stopping?" I asked.

"This is it!" Vicky exclaimed in her jazzed-up hypershrill "gonna dance the night away" voice.

I looked around there were no other cars or people. Puzzled and a little concerned I asked, "Yes, but what is it?"

Vicki was already hauling out her backpack. "Let's go!"

"OK," I murmured, not reassured. I hardly knew her, and now I was in her hands completely.

It was late in the afternoon when we threw our packs over the fence, then the ice chest of beer. It crushed the golden wheat that swayed in the breeze. We dragged ourselves through the middle strand of the barbed wire, hoping not to be snagged, and walked across the field, carrying the ice chest and wearing our packs on our backs. As we struggled along, I noticed a tingling sensation on the soles of my feet, similar to the aftershocks of an earthquake, but not alarming. In fact, the feeling beckoned me to move forward, to find out more.

Vicki became uncharacteristically quiet. She was visibly changing from a high-maintenance, high-energy nurse to something soft, soulful, and animal-like. The vibration I'd noticed began to climb up my legs, into my knees, into my pelvis, and along the base of my spine. We were moving closer to the vibration. The closer we got, the further up my spine it climbed until it reached into my heart. The rhythm of the vibration had taken over and synchronized with my heart, touching it, awakening me to a long ago forgotten place deep in my core.

I asked Vicki, "What is that pulsing?"

"It's the Mother's heart beat, the drum. Welcome home!" she sighed, whispering not just to me, but to herself.

"Perfect," the wind whispered back to me.

As we came to the edge of the woods, the sound of the drum grew louder, then we heard the voices of the singers. They were singing songs in the old language, which I understood, not really knowing how this could be.

This powwow was a celebration of the People. All of the People and their talents and their crafts—weaving, drum making, pipe making, and more were celebrated. It was an opportunity for the young children to learn from their elders, to learn the songs and the dances, to use the tribe's language. From the first beat of the drum, I knew this Way or rendition of this was my Way, my Home.

We finally reached the other participants in the powwow, and found Vicki's mom. She was dressed in doeskin the same color as her dark skin. She hurried toward us and embraced Vicki, then hugged me with a mother's love. Her dark brown eyes sparkled with joy, and she said she was thrilled that we were there. It seemed that until Vicki had met me, she had lost interest in her mother's traditions. As she put it, "Vicki has been more interested in money and fame than bathing in the roots of her tradition."

I was envious of Vicki, her relationship with her mom, and her identified heritage. They knew their tribe. They knew where they came from, where they had been, and what they needed to do to stay the course. Now I understood this deep ache that had been with me from my first memory. I ached for this knowing of family. I ached for my tribe.

We were on Indian time, of course. This was my first introduction to Indian time. My style was to know when things were going to start and when things were going to end. This was my first taste of allowing things to unfold naturally and to relinquish control. Many of the family members and some of the chiefs had not arrived yet. Vicki and I wandered around to some of the other tents to find cousins distant and relatives. I was surprised when I walked up to meet one of Vicki's cousins. He was half-dressed, making repairs to his costume for his dance. He was what is known as a "fancy dancer." Fancy dancing is a contest dance, one of the exciting and beautiful dances done at powwows. The term "fancy dance" is derived from the intricate regalia and complicated dance moves. He talked with us about the eagle feathers on his costume, and told us with a smirk, "Only Native Americans are allowed to own the feathers of birds of prey, and they are not allowed to kill the bird to get the feathers. They're only allowed to find them on the ground."

He had mounds of eagle feathers in his car for his costume, and his car bumper stickers proclaimed, "America Love It or Give It Back! Dancing to the Beat of a Different Drum. This Land Is NOT Your Land!" I understood the sentiment, but I was relieved that these people saw the Indian in my face and welcomed me. Still, I was not official since I was not on The Roll. The Roll is the list of Native Americans who have proven they have at least one-sixteenth Native American blood. I wanted this proof, but the holder of the information was my dad, and I knew I couldn't get it from him.

As time rolled on, we saw a number of singers and dancers who performed for the white people who paid to see them. The real show finally began after the white people went home. It was after midnight when most of the chiefs showed up with their families. I felt honored being there, like I had just been given the perfect birthday gift after years of waiting. It was so wonderful to be a part of watching the People dance.

The tribe voted a young woman as princess to represent them in other powwow competitions. The powwow princess is selected for a variety of cultural factors including her ability as a dancer and the quality of her outfit. This powwow princess was around eighteen years of age. She was wearing a dress handmade by her mother and grandmother, white doeskin with turquoise and red beading depicting her commitment to the red way and to the United States. The beading was in rows of ten that went around her and in between the rows were beaded flowers with humming-birds feeding from them. The dress flowed down to fringe that brushed the ground as she danced. Buried in the fringe were tiny jingle cones that were supposed to scare away bad spirits. Her moccasins were beaded to match her dress. A crown of deer hide and natural stones rested on top of her head, and her black hair fell to her waist in a braid. She led the procession of dancers into the ring around the drum for the opening ceremony. I felt in awe and envy of the history she carried inside of her. I wanted the acknowledgment of my history.

As the evening kept rolling, I was the only person left sitting on the rickety bleachers they'd moved in from some Little League ball field. My heart kept sneaking closer to the drum. The closer I got to it, the more peace washed over me. I wanted to dance, but I dared not ask. Vicki's mom told me to observe this time and not ask too many questions or I would be ostracized. This was my first dose of patience, with many more lessons to come.

I saw so many kinds of dances. The young women danced the butterfly dance, which was swift with high steps, and they swirled like butterflies, their feet lifting off the ground. The older women danced a slow-patterned yet soulful meditative dance around the drum. The fancy dancers and eagle dancers painted their faces and upper bodies with their personal and tribe symbols. They wore all of their feathers, bells, and headdresses, and danced quickly and wildly, calling the spirits of the buffalo, deer, eagle, and hawk. Often they simply whirled and called in spirits to heal and to help. Dances were dedicated to the Great Spirit along with a dedication to a tribe member who was serving in the military and for family members who were ill. The dances are prayers in action.

I sat, and I watched. I watched, and I sat. I was in a trance when Vicki's mom came up to me, and handed me her guest shawl beaded in green and purple. This was my invitation to dance. I was so honored I couldn't speak. I knew it meant I was accepted as an adopted sister of the tribe. She wrapped the cloak of sisterhood around my shoulders, took me by the hand, and we walked down to the inner circle around the drum with the other women. My feet moved to the music as if the dance had been unearthed from my DNA. I danced, and moved closer to the drum. I danced, and I moved closer and closer to my Heart. I danced, and I moved closer and closer to my Home. I danced and I danced and I found my Mother. I danced and I danced, and I found my Self.

EPILOGUE

We've journeyed together in this book, traveling through pathways of remembered moments and thinking about loved ones who may exist only in memory. We've seen that writing is not only a powerful tool for healing, but also a way to enjoy the fruits of your creativity and imagination. Now that you've begun a few stories, you may wonder: "How do I keep writing?"

Merely thinking about writing—or procrastinating by cleaning the house instead of writing—leads to empty pages and a feeling that we've let ourselves down. That's why I recommend that you make a plan.

A Writing Life Plan

Many of my students and clients find that the first step in continuing to write is to create or join a community of writers that understands your goals and shares your passion.

Writing Groups

A writing group can be a great support system. You could join any group of people who are dedicated and serious about writing, but keep in mind that the process of writing a fictional story may be somewhat different from writing a memoir.

Also, always take the feedback and criticism you may receive in a group with a grain of salt. Some of my students have heard such judgments as, "That (abusive or traumatic) story can't be true, such things can never happen." Or, "Come on, you're exaggerating." Even worse, "That's crazy, how could you let that happen to you?"

Be cautious when sharing stories about violence, mental illness, abuse, and other controversial issues. People who haven't been in therapy or who are unaware of the complex dynamics involved in such situations may find it difficult to understand irrational behavior or "dark" stories. They may be frightened by them, or your story may remind them of their own unconscious issues.

If you find yourself in an unsafe group, look for another one where there are rules and boundaries, and some kind of psychological insight about the range of human behavior. Memoir writers need a sense of safety and even confidentiality in a writing group. I always ask that the stories shared in the group be held in confidence, which helps the writers to feel safer to disclose secrets and revealing stories.

Your writing group can usually provide more objective feedback about your work than friends or family can. Some family members won't be able to absorb your journey into healing because it upsets them to see you in pain. They might even suggest that you give up writing, which is not the kind of feedback that supports your writing life. Others may chide you for staying in the past. "Aren't you over that yet?" Or worse, "You're just wallowing in misery by writing about it."

Keeping a Writing Journal

Because healing is the purpose of writing your memoir, you'll find it especially helpful to keep a journal about the progress of your memoir. You may record new topics, fears, or worries about your family's responses. You might chronicle your stories, plan your time line, and freewrite memories that come up.

As the past makes its way into your consciousness and even into your dreams, you'll probably encounter raw emotions and deep feelings you may not have been aware of until now. Part of memoir writing is confronting the past and your various selves face-to-face. Writing about your feelings and your progress with your project will help you to maintain emotional balance and reach a deeper level of understanding.

Planning Your Writing Life

Writing requires reflection, time, and a routine. When my students say, "I didn't have time to write this week. I was dreaming and thinking about the story, but I don't have anything to show for it," I assure them they've already done some of their work.

A memoir writer needs to spend time thinking, dreaming, musing, and keeping a journal. A story must live inside you, and you must learn to listen deeply and with full presence in order to bring it out of your body, like a birthing. Accept your process and yourself during this stage.

Because everyone's creative process works differently, you need to do what feels comfortable. Set a goal for when you hope to finish, and count backwards from there. Figure out how many hours a week you can write while taking care of the rest of your life. Some people work best with a schedule, and others need to write when inspired. To get a whole memoir finished in a reasonable length of time—let's say within a year or so for the first draft—you need to take into account several factors.

Some writers set impossible goals: "I'll write every day for four or five hours." Then they become unhappy with themselves when they can't keep up. Most people don't have four or five hours every day when they can write, so be realistic.

Keep in mind that

1. While you're writing your memoir, you're learning to write a book, a daunting task in itself.
2. You're processing your life on a deep emotional level while you're writing, so you need to allow time for it.
3. Even a book-length memoir can be completed with steady but brief bursts of writing. You'll be amazed at what you can accomplish in fifteen-minute bursts of writing. Set measurable and realistic goals. You'll find your own natural rhythm and patterns that work best. You can extend the amount of time as you get into the routine of writing.

Writers need to create accountability and to structure their writing life so their writing time is a priority. The writers I know who don't create accountability end up frustrated with their writing progress. Setting a certain number of pages to complete for your writing group or coach creates an expectation that can help you get your work done.

The Importance of a Positive Attitude

Having a positive attitude as well as measurable goals are good ways to create a workable writing life.

1. Remind yourself that you've dedicated yourself to writing and make it a priority. Set up specific writing dates with yourself.
2. Approach the writing with a beginner's mind: simply put your pen to the page and write. It doesn't matter how much you write or what you write, allow the pen to move in a freewrite. You can edit it later and shape it into a vignette if you wish.

3. If you write only when you feel happy and inspired, you may miss the opportunity to allow the writing to help you feel better if you're writing a "dark" story. Keep the writing brief, and then plan something else for your day.

4. Remember to balance writing about painful subjects with writing about the happy times in your life. Alternate the dark and light stories.

5. Nurture yourself. Find ways to reward yourself when you have completed your writing for the day—a favorite movie, new book, a frothy cappuccino, planting flowers, or a date with a friend.

Writing a memoir is an act of courage, love, and inspiration. Through writing we are brought deeply into ourselves, into the heart of our lives and our feelings, and the meaning we make about everything we have experienced. If you translate your memories into scenes and story, they will change you. The stories become your teacher.

When you write, you may discover new aspects of yourself, you may find new memories, insights, and even feelings you were not aware of before. Writing a memoir is a transformational journey into the unknown, satisfying and rewarding beyond measure.

Pick up your pen today. Be brave. Begin your memoir now.

RESOURCES

Web Sites and Blogs

National Association of Memoir Writers: www.namw.org

Memories and Memoirs: www.memoriesandmemoirs.com

Memory Writer's Network: www.memorywritersnetwork.com

The Heart and Craft of Life Writing: www.heartandcraft.blog spot.com

Turning Memories into Memoirs: www.turningmemories.com

Kathleen Adams, Center for Journal Therapy: www.journal therapy.com

Block Buster Plots: www.blockbusterplots.com

Suite 101 Link for Memoirs: www.writingmemoirs.suite101. com

Self-Help Healing Arts Journal: www.self-help-healing-arts-journal.com

Creative Writing Blog: www.creativewritingblog.org

Kim's Craft Blog: kimscraftblog.blogspot.com

Moonbridge Blog: www.moonbridgeblog.blogspot.com

100 Memoirs: www.100memoirs.com

One Year of Writing and Healing: www.oneyearofwritingand healing.com

Absolute Write: www.absolutewrite.com

Christina Baldwin: Website: www.peerspirit.com; Blog: http://storycatcher.net/wordpress

Sheila Bender: www.writingitreal.com

Lucia Capacchione—Creative Journal Expressive Arts Certification Training: www.luciac.com; www.visioningcoach.org; www.visioningcoach.blogspot.com

Dr. James Pennebaker: www.psy.utexas.edu/pennebaker

Matthew Lieberman: www.lieberman.socialpsychology.org

Bessel van der Kolk: www.traumacenter.org

Marina Nemat: www.marinanemat.com

Sites for Women

Women's Memoirs: www.womensmemoirs.com

Story Circle Network: www.storycircle.org; www.storycircle.typepad.com

International Women's Writing Guild: www.iwwg.org

National Association of Women Writers: www.naww.org

The Business of Writing

Poets and Writers: www.pw.org

Writer's Digest: www.writersdigest.com

The Writer: www.writermag.com

Association of Author's Representatives (literary agents): www.aaronline.org

Self-publishing resources:

Logical Expressions: www.logicalexpressions.com

Dan Poynter: www.parapublishing.com

RECOMMENDED READING

Adams, Kathleen	*Journal to the Self*
Alderson, Martha	*Blockbuster Plots*
Allende, Isabel	*Paula*
Allison, Dorothy	*Two or Three Things I Know for Sure*
Angelou, Maya	*I Know Why the Caged Bird Sings*
Armstrong, Karen	*The Spiral Staircase*
Baldwin, James	*Notes of a Native Son*
Bender, Sheila	*Writing and Publishing Personal Essays*
Ball, Edward	*Slaves in the Family*
Butler, Matilda; Bonnett, Kendra	*Rosie's Daughters*
Arenas, Reinaldo	*Before Night Falls*
Baker, Russell	*Growing Up*
Balakian, Peter	*Black Dog of Fate*
Barrington, Judith	*Writing the Memoir: From Truth to Art; Lifesaving*
Birkerts, Sven	*The Art of Time in Memoir: Then, Again*

Bateson, Catherine	*Composing a Life; Through a Daughter's Eye*
Bolton, Gillie	*The Therapeutic Potential of Creative Writing*
Bragg, Rick	*All Over but the Shoutin'; Ava's Man*
Brautigan, Ianthe	*You Can't Catch Death*
Brittain, Vera	*Testament of Youth*
Burroughs, Augusten	*Running with Scissors*
Capacchione, Lucia	*Recovery of Your Inner Child*
Chernin, Kim	*In My Mother's House (and other works)*
Colette	*My Mother's House; Sido*
Conroy, Frank	*Stop Time*
Conroy, Pat	*My Losing Season*
Conway, Jill Ker	*When Memory Speaks; The Road from Coorain*
Dalai Lama	*The Art of Happiness*
Danticat, Edwidge	*Brother, I'm Dying*
Day, Dorothy	*The Long Loneliness*
DeBeauvoir, Simone	*Memoirs of a Dutiful Daughter (first of a three-part autobiography)*
De Salvo, Louise	*Writing as a Way of Healing*
Didion, Joan	*The Year of Magical Thinking*
Eggers, David	*A Heartbreaking Work of Staggering Genius; Zeitoun*
Elliot, T. S.	*The Four Quartets*
Epstein, Helen	*Where She Came From*
Fiori, Neil	*The Now Habit: A Strategic Program for Overcoming Procrastination and Enjoying Guilt-Free Play*
Fox, John	*Poetic Medicine*
Fremont, Helen	*After Long Silence*

Gebler, Carlo	*My Father and I*
Gilmore, Mikal	*Shot in the Heart*
Goldberg, Natalie	*Writing Down the Bones (and other books)*
Gordon, Mary	*Shadow Man*
Gornick, Vivian	*Fierce Attachments; The Situation and the Story*
Gunther, John	*Death Be Not Proud*
Hampl, Patricia	*Tell Me True: Memoir, History, and Writing a Life; The Florist's Daughter*
Harrison, Catherine	*The Kiss*
Heilbrun, Carolyn	*Writing a Woman's Life*
Hemingway, Ernest	*A Moveable Feast*
Hoffman, Eva	*Lost in Translation*
Jamison, Kay	*An Unquiet Mind*
Jung, Carl	*Memories, Dreams, Reflections*
Kamenetz, Rodger	*Terra Infirma: A Memoir of My Mother's Life in Mine*
Karr, Mary	*The Liar's Club; Cherry*
Kaysen, Suzanne	*Girl, Interrupted*
Kingston, Maxine Hong	*Woman Warrior*
L'Engle, Madeleine	*The Summer of the Great-Grandmother*
Lamott, Anne	*Traveling Mercies; Bird by Bird*
Lanchester, John	*Family Romance: A Love Story*
Lauck, Jennifer	*Blackbird; Still Waters*
Lawrence, T. E.	*Seven Pillars of Wisdom*
Ledoux, Denis	*Turning Memories into Memoirs*
Lukeman, Noah	*The Plot Thickens*
MacDonald, Michael	*All Souls: A Family Story from Southie*
Mason, Bobbie Ann	*Clear Springs*
Mairs, Nancy	*Remembering the Bone House*

Martin, Steve	*Born Standing up*
Maynard, Isabelle	*China Dreams: Growing Up Jewish in Tientsin*
Maynard, Joyce	*At Home in the World*
McBride, James	*The Color of Water: A Black Man's Tribute to His White Mother*
McCarthy, Mary	*Memories of a Catholic Girlhood*
McCourt, Frank	*Angela's Ashes; Tis*
Mead, Margaret	*Blackberry Winter*
Merton, Thomas	*Seven Story Mountain*
Nabakov, Vladimir	*Speak, Memory*
Nafisi, Azar	*Reading Lolita in Tehran; Things I've Been Silent About*
Neruda, Pablo	*Memoirs*
Norris, Kathleen	*Amazing Grace; Cloister Walk*
O'Faolain, Nuala	*Are You Somebody?; Almost There*
Ondaatje, Michael	*Running in the Family*
Pennebaker, James	*Opening Up: The Healing Power of Expressing Emotions*
Pham, Andrew X.	*Catfish and Mandala*
Oz, Amos	*Tales of Love and Darkness*
Perel, Solomon	*Europa, Europa*
Polking, Kirk	*Writing Family Histories and Memoirs*
Rainer, Tristine	*Your Life as Story: Writing the New Autobiography*
Reichl, Ruth	*Tender at the Bone; Comfort Me with Apples*
Rhodes, Richard	*A Hole in the World*
Rosenfeld, Jordan	*Make a Scene*
Santos, John Phillip	*Places Left Unfinished at the Time of Creation*
Sarton, May	*Journal of a Solitude*

Scott-Maxwell, Florida	*The Measure of My Days*
Sebold, Alice	*Lucky*
See, Carolyn	*Dreaming*
Silverman, Sue William	*Because I Remember Terror Father, I Remember You; Fearless Confessions*
Stegner, Wallace	*Wolf Willow*
Thomas, Abigail	*Thinking About Memoir*
Ueland, Brenda	*If You Want to Write*
Umrigar, Thirty	*First Darling of the Morning*
Villasenor, Victor	*Thirteen Senses*
Walker, Rebecca	*Black, White, and Jewish*
Weisel, Elie	*The Night Trilogy*
Welty, Eudora	*One Writer's Beginnings*
Williams, Terry Tempest	*Leap; Refuge: An Unnatural History of Family and Place*
Wolff, Geoffrey	*The Duke of Deception*
Wolff, Tobias	*This Boy's Life; Pharaoh's Army*
Woolf, Virginia	*Moments of Being; To the Lighthouse*
Wright, Richard	*Black Boy*

Novelists who draw on autobiographical material—too many to name, but here are a few:

Dorothy Allison	*Bastard Out of Carolina*
Willa Cather	*My Antonia*
Sandra Cisneros	*The House on Mango Street*
Charles Dickens	*David Copperfield*
Ernest Hemingway	*For Whom the Bell Tolls*
F. Scott Fitzgerald	*The Great Gatsby*
Pat Conroy	*Prince of Tides*

Jumpa Lahiri	*The Namesake*
Harper Lee	*To Kill a Mockingbird*
Tim O'Brien	*The Things They Carried*
Irene Nemirovsky	*Suite Française*
John Steinbeck	*East of Eden*
Marcel Proust	*Remembrance of Things Past*
Leo Tolstoy	*Family Happiness*

READER'S GUIDE

1. Some people want to write a memoir to gain a new perspective on the past, and others to share their story with family. What are your reasons for writing your memoir? Whom do you want to read it? What do you hope the audience will learn from reading about your life?

2. When you write a memoir, you draw upon family history and the historical context of ancestors. In what period of history do your stories take place? Which family members would you like to interview as part of your research? Are there questions you feel you should stay away from; if so, why?

3. Choosing major turning points helps you to focus on the overwhelming number of memories and events. What turning points are the most significant in your life? How do they fit in with the history of your family? When do important events on your time line coincide with significant historical events? You might want to write about where your time line intersects with the larger time line of history.

4. Writing a memoir is a deeply psychological process, revealing the family to the writer in often surprising ways. What role did you play in your family? Who in your family has the most power and how do they show it? How did the family rules,

roles, and myths help you to have, or keep you from having, the life you wanted?

5. Most people encounter "dark nights of the soul" on their life journeys. What have you learned from the challenging times in your life? How have they shaped who you are now? Be sure to put them on your time line. Write about before and after, and what you learned from these moments.

6. All writers wrestle with their inner critics. How does your inner critic stop you? What are your critic's messages? Discuss them with your writing group. Answer back with righteous entitlement to claim your right to write.

7. Stories have a structure: how we're drawn in (Act I); complications and developments of a story (Act II); the satisfaction of an emotionally complete ending (Act III). How would you divide your life (or your memoir) into three acts? What is the climax? The conflicts? The resolution (of your story, not your life).

8. Every memoir deserves its rightful home somewhere, whether it's photocopied for family, self-published, or distributed around the world. How do you envision the audience for your memoir? How would you summarize the theme of your memoir in one sentence? What kind of publishing goals do you have? What is the title of your memoir?

9. A great deal of evidence shows how writing can be helpful as a healing process. What do you want to heal in your life? Have you experienced healing through writing? What has changed for you? What are your goals for healing now? How do you envision your future self?

10. Meditation is a way to bring a calm focus to your writing life. Have you explored relaxation and meditation as part of your writing life? Try relaxing into the dream world of memory for ten minutes, and then freewrite afterward what you notice. Practice this several times a week.

11. Affirmations are useful ways to counteract negative voices and attitudes. What three affirmations do you think would be most helpful to create a positive environment for your writing? Write them on cards and put them around the house to remind you of a new attitude.

12. Creating a structure for your writing life helps the creative process—the unconscious mind makes a "date" to show up for you. Write down a schedule—it can be fifteen minutes three times a week—when you will invite your creativity to play with you.

BIBLIOGRAPHY

Adams, Kathleen. *Journal to the Self*. New York: Warner Books, 1990.

————. *The Way of the Journal*. Lutherville, MD: Sidran Press, 1998.

————. *The Write Way to Wellness*. Lakewood, CO: Center for Journal Therapy, 2000.

————. Interview by the National Association of Memoir Writers, April 23, 2009.

Albert, Susan Wittig. *Writing from Life: Telling Your Soul's Story*. New York: Tarcher, 1997.

Allende, Isabel. *Paula*. New York: HarperCollins, 1995.

Allison, Dorothy. *Bastard Out of Carolina*. New York: Dutton, 1992.

————. *Two or Three Things I Know for Sure* New York: Penguin, 1995.

Armstrong, Karen. *The Spiral Staircase*. New York: Knopf, 2004.

Baldwin, Christina. *Life's Companion: Journal Writing as a Spiritual Quest*. New York: Bantam, 1998.

Bennett, Hal Zia. *Writing Spiritual Books*. Makawao, HI: Inner Ocean, 2004.

————. *Storycatcher*. Novato, CA: New World Library, 2005.

Black, Claudia. *It Will Never Happen to Me*. New York: Ballantine, 1981.

Brande, Dorothea. *Becoming a Writer*. Reprint, with a foreword by John Gardner. New York: Tarcher, 1981. (Originally published 1943.)

Burroughs, Augusten. *Running with Scissors*. New York: Picador, 2002.

Butler, Matilda; Bonnett, Kendra. *Rosie's Daughters "The First Women To" Generation Tell Their Stories*. Berkeley, CA: Two Bridges Press, 2007.

Cameron, Julia. *The Artist's Way: A Spiritual Path to Higher Creativity*. Tenth anniversary edition. New York: Tarcher, 2002.

Capacchione, Lucia. *The Power of Your Other Hand*. Second edition. Franklin Lakes, NJ: Career Press, 2001.

———. *The Creative Journal*. Second edition. Franklin Lakes, NJ: Career Press, 2002.

———. Interview with the National Association of Memoir Writers, 2009.

Conroy, Pat. *My Losing Season*. New York: Random House, 2002.

Conway, Jill Ker. *When Memory Speaks*. New York: Vintage Books, 1998.

Dalai Lama. *The Art of Happiness*. New York: Riverhead Books, 1998.

Dandicat, Edwidge. *Brother, I'm Dying*. New York: Vintage Books, 2004.

DeSalvo, Louise. *Writing as a Way of Healing: How Telling Our Stories Transforms Our Lives*. Boston: Beacon Press, 2000.

Didion, Joan. *The Year of Magical Thinking*. New York: Vintage Books, 2005.

Dillard, Annie. To Fashion a Text. In *Inventing the Truth: The Art and Craft of Memoir*, edited and with a memoir and introduction by William Zinsser. Boston: Houghton Mifflin, 1987.

Elliot. T. S. *The Four Quartets*. Orlando, FL: Harcourt Brace, 1971.

Gardner, John. *The Art of Fiction*. New York: Vintage Books, 1983.

Gordon, Mary. *Circling My Mother*. New York: Pantheon Books, 2007.

Haley, Alex. *Roots*. New York: Doubleday, 1976.

Hampl, Patricia. *The Florist's Daughter*. New York: Houghton Mifflin, 2007.

Harrison, Katharine. *The Kiss*. New York: Avon Books, 1997.

Herman, Judith. *Trauma and Recovery*. New York: Basic Books, 1992.

Hanh, Thich Nhat. *Teachings on Love*. Berkeley, CA: Parallax Press, 1997.

Jamison, Kay. *An Unquiet Mind*. New York: Vintage Books, 1996.

Janov, Arthur. *Primal Healing*. Franklin Lakes, NJ: New Page Books, 2006.

Kaysen, Susan. *Girl, Interrupted*. New York: Vintage Books, 1994.

Kien, Nguyen. *The Unwanted*. New York: Little, Brown & Company, 2001.

King, Laurie. Gain Without Pain? Expressive Writing and Self-Regulation. In *The Writing Cure: How Expressive Writing Promotes Health and Emotional Well-Being*, eds., Stephen J. Lepore and Joshua M. Smyth. Washington, DC: American Psychological Association, 2002.

Kingston, Maxine Hong. *The Woman Warrior: Memoirs of a Girlhood Among Ghosts*. New York: Vintage Books, 1975.

Lamott, Anne. *Traveling Mercies*. New York: Pantheon Random House, 1999.

———. *Grace (Eventually) Thoughts on Faith*. New York: Penguin Group, 2007.

Lauck, Jennifer. *Blackbird*. New York: Simon & Schuster, 2000.

———. *Still Waters*. New York: Washington Square Press, 2001.

Ledoux, Denis. *Turning Memories into Memoirs*. Lisbon Falls, ME: Soleil Press, 1991.

LeDoux, Joseph. *The Emotional Brain*. New York: Touchstone, 1996.

Lepore, Stephen J., and Joshua M. Smyth, eds. *The Writing Cure: How Expressive Writing Promotes Health and Emotional Well-Being*. Washington, DC: American Psychological Association, 2002.

Levine, Peter A. *Waking the Tiger: Healing Trauma*. Berkeley, CA: North Atlantic Books. 1997.

Lieberman, Matthew. "Putting Feelings into Words Produces Therapeutic Effects in the Brain." 2007. Available from www.college.ucla.edu/news/07/feelings-into-words.html.

Lyon, Elizabeth. *A Writers' Guide to Fiction*. New York: Berkley, 2004.

Mahler, Margaret. *The Psychological Birth of the Human Infant*. New York: Basic Books, 1975.

Maslow, Abraham. *Toward a New Psychology of Being*. New York: Wiley, 1998.

Masterson, James. *The Real Self*. New York: The Free Press, 1988.

McBride, James. *The Color of Water*. New York: Riverhead Books, 1996.

McDonald, Michael. *All Souls: A Family Story from Southie*. Boston: Beacon Press, 1999.

Metzger, Deena. *Writing for Your Life*. New York: HarperCollins, 1992.

Miller, Alice. *For Your Own Good*. New York: Farrar, Strauss and Giroux, 1983.

————. *The Drama of the Gifted Child*. New York: Basic Books, 1997.

————. *The Truth Will Set You Free*. New York: Basic Books, 2001.

Murdock, Maurine. *Unreliable Truth*. Berkeley, CA: Seal Press, 2003.

Myers, Linda Joy. *Don't Call Me Mother: Breaking the Chain of Mother-Daughter Abandonment*. Berkeley, CA: Two Bridges Press, 2005.

Nemat, Marina. *Prisoner of Tehran*. New York: Free Press, 2007.

Nin, Anaïs. *The Diary of Anaïs Nin*. Vol. II (March 1937). New York: Swallow Press, 1967.

Norris, Kathleen. *Cloister Walk*. New York: Riverhead Books, Penguin-Putnam, 1996.

O'Faolain, Nuala. *Are You Somebody?* New York: Holt and Company, 1996.

Oz, Amos. *Tales of Love and Darkness*. Orlando, FL: Harcourt Brace, 2003.

Pennebaker, James W. *Opening Up: The Healing Power of Expressing Emotions*. New York: The Guilford Press, 1990.

————. Personal conversation with author, February 4, 2002, in Austin, Texas.

————. *Writing to Heal*. Oakland, CA: New Harbinger, 2004.

————. Interview with the National Association of Memoir Writers, April 23, 2009.

Pennebaker, James W., and Janel D. Seagal. "Forming a Story: The Health Benefits of Narrative." *Journal of Clinical Psychology*, 1999, 55 (10): 1243–1254.

Pham, Andrew. *Catfish and Mandala*. New York: Picador, 1999.

Rainer, Tristine. *The New Diary: Your Life as Story*. New York: Tarcher, 1997.

————. *Your Life as Story: Discovering the "New Autobiography" and Writing Memoir as Literature*. New York: Tarcher, 1998.

Rhodes, Richard. *A Hole in the World*. New York: Touchstone, 1990.

Rothschild, Babette. *The Body Remembers: The Psychophysiology of Trauma and Trauma Treatment*. New York: Norton, 2000.

Salon.com. Jeniffer Lauck Interview. http://www.salon.com/books/feature/2001/12/12/lauck/print.html. Accessed June 28, 2002.

Sebold, Alice. *Lucky*. New York: Scribner, 1999.

————. *The Lovely Bones*. New York: Little, Brown & Company, 2002.

Siegel, Daniel. *The Developing Mind*. NewYork: The Guilford Press, 1999.

Siegel, Daniel J., and Marion F. Solomon, eds. *Healing Trauma: Attachment, Mind, Body, and Brain*. NewYork: W. W. Norton, 2003.

Smyth, J., A. Stone, A. Hurewitz, and A. Kaell."Writing About Stressful Events Produces Symptom Reduction in Asthmatics and Rheumatoid Arthritics: A Randomized Trial." *Journal of the American Medical Association*, 1999, *281*, 1304–1309.

Suzuki, Shunryu. *Zen Mind, Beginner's Mind*. New York: Weatherhill, 1973.

Tolstoy, Leo. *Anna Karenina*. New York: Penguin, 2000. (Originally published 1877.)

Ueland, Brenda. *If You Want to Write: A Book About Art, Independence and Spirit*. Saint Paul, MN: Graywolf Press, 1987.

Wakefield, Dan. *The Story of Your Life: Writing a Spiritual Autobiography*. Boston: Beacon Press, 1990.

Walls, Jeannette. *The Glass Castle*. New York: Scribner, 2005.

Weldon, Michele. *Writing to Save Your Life*. Center City, MI: Hazelden, 2001.

Welty, Eudora. *One Writer's Beginnings*. Cambridge: Harvard University Press, 1983.

van der Kolk, Bessel. *Traumatic Stress*. New York: The Guildford Press, 1996.

————. "In Terror's Grip: Healing the Ravages of Trauma." *Cerebrum*, 2002, *4*, 34–50. New York: The Dana Foundation. Available from www.traumacenter.org/products/publications.

Wolff, Tobias. *This Boy's Life*. New York: Harper Perennial, 1989.

Woolf, Virginia. *Moments of Being*. Orlando, FL: Harvest Books, 1976.

————. *A Sketch of the Past—In Moments of Being*. Orlando: Harcourt Brace Jovanovich, 1985.

ABOUT THE AUTHOR

L inda Joy Myers, Ph.D., is the president of the National Association of Memoir Writers. For the last thirty years she has been a practicing therapist in Berkeley, California. She is the author of an award-winning memoir, *Don't Call Me Mother: Breaking the Chain of Mother-Daughter Abandonment*. Linda received her MFA from Mills College and has won prizes for her work in fiction, nonfiction, and poetry. Her teaching experience includes John F. Kennedy University and Argosy University, where she taught marriage and family therapy. Linda has trained therapists in using autobiography techniques with their clients for therapeutic healing.

Through her workshops, coaching, and speaking engagements presented nationally and internationally, Linda integrates the principles of healing and creativity and inspires people to find the courage to write their stories. She lives in the San Francisco Bay Area.

Index

Printed in the United States of America
ED-10-19-12